# QUIT YOUR DAY JOB

**A REAL ESTATE BLUEPRINT TO REPLACE YOUR PAYCHECK WITH RENTAL INCOME**

## JUAN PABLO

*Quit Your Day Job: A Real Estate Blueprint to Replace Your Paycheck with Rental Income*

Copyright © 2018, 2019 by Juan Pablo

*Second Edition:* December 2019

All rights reserved. No part of this book may be reproduced in any form by any electronic or mechanical means including photocopying, recording, or information storage and retrieval without permission in writing from the author, except for the inclusion of brief quotations in a review.

The information in this book is not meant to replace the advice of a certified professional. Please consult a licensed advisor in matters relating to your livelihood including your health, both mentally and physically, financial endeavors, business ventures, family affairs, educational goals, and spiritual pursuits.

If you choose to attempt any of the methods outlined in this book, the author and publisher advises you to take full responsibility for your safety and know your limits. The author and publisher are not liable for any damages or negative consequences from any treatment, action, application, or preparation to any person reading or following the information in this book.

Neither the publisher nor the author shall be liable for any physical, psychological, emotional, financial, or commercial damages, including but not limited to special incidental, consequential or other damages to the readers of this book.

The content of each chapter is the sole expression and opinion of its author and not necessarily that of the publisher. No warranties or guarantees are expressed or implied by the publisher's choice to include any of the content in this publication.

ISBN No. 978-1-671-28473-9

PRINTED AND BOUND IN THE UNITED STATES OF AMERICA

# What Reviewers Are Saying

"Omg Juan, in less than 24 hours, I completed the book. It was amazing. It contains so much valuable information. It should be sold in universities as a $100 text book! I sat down and really determined my financial freedom numbers. I have some work to put in! I determined that I'd need to purchase 5 more units per year for the next 5 years to be completely financially free. I really enjoyed the sections on PILE, Master Lease Options and the Deal Finders and Deal Analysis. Those sections I feel were most useful for me. I don't want to give too much away, but the Daily Affirmations and the end were very encouraging. I have so many underlines and sticky notes in the book so I can go back to make reference. This book is on its way to being a best seller. Excellent job, and thank you again."

–A.C.

"Juan Pablo did an excellent job writing this book. He lays out step by step what you need to do in order to achieve financial freedom in many aspects of real estate so it does not matter if you are dead broke or have cash ready to go. It is a very easy read with TONS of helpful information. However this book is for people beginning in real estate...seasoned investors will know most of the information that being said this book was intended for people just beginning but even myself having a couple years investing in real estate under my belt I still took away quite a few golden nuggets. Absolutely worth the money!!"   –A.C.

---

"GET YOUR LIFE TOGETHER!! Juan Pablo tells you how: how to fix your credit, how to buy your first multi unit property. IT TAKES TIME TO GET IT TOGETHER. But don't give up! It took him 2 years to get his credit fixed and save up for his first deal. Just do what he says, even if you don't become a real estate investor you will have better credit to get a house, a motorcycle, a credit card, a plane ticket, etc."   –Aurisa

"This book has been what I needed! It serves as a tremendous motivator in investing in real estate. I love how Juan Pablo mixes his back story with lessons learned and facts. This book is a great do's and don't for real estate investing." —*Junito*

---

"This is an awesome book for beginners. I found Juan on YouTube and I've been hooked on real estate ever since. This book contains so much info and doesn't cost no more than 1-2 hours of work. It's well worth it! You'll honestly be 10 steps ahead of other beginners after reading this book. Thank you Juan Pablo and god bless you my friend." —*JJ*

---

"This book is a Must Read to add to your collection. It helps you to gain confidence in the Real Estate market the more you read it."
—*Saudia Lynn*

Go to https://info.100percentfinanced.com/blog-subscription to get free tips on real estate and more.

# Special Thanks

Thanks goes out to God, who changed my poor life into a great one. Thanks goes out to Mom and Rose for providing me with books and the opportunities that changed my life. Thanks to the Richdad NYC community for providing me with instruction to quit my day job, and for inspiring me to convert this knowledge into a business that has changed the lives of many. Thanks to everyone in the 100 Percent Financed community for making life as an online entrepreneur much less painful than it could be. Without you all, this book would not be possible.

Last, and certainly not least, special thanks to you. I hope you find value from this book, and if you find value, please buy a family member, friend, or colleague their own copy to pay it forward-each one teach one. Speaking of paying it forward, 100% of the profits generated from the sale of the printed copies of this book, as well as all my other books are donated to charity.

# Table of Contents

Introduction . . . . . . . . . . . . . . . . . . . . . . . . . . . . .1

Road to Financial Freedom . . . . . . . . . . . . . . . . . . .9

First Roadblock: Fixing Bad Credit . . . . . . . . . . . .45

Running Out of Gas: Feeling Burned Out . . . . . . .55

Second Roadblock: Running Out of Gas Money . . .69

The First M: The Model . . . . . . . . . . . . . . . . . . . .87

The Second M: The Market . . . . . . . . . . . . . . . . .109

The Third M: The Money . . . . . . . . . . . . . . . . . .117

Deal Finders . . . . . . . . . . . . . . . . . . . . . . . . . . . .131

Deal Analysis . . . . . . . . . . . . . . . . . . . . . . . . . . .139

Wholesaling Real Estate Without Cash or Credit . .151

Wash, Rinse & Repeat . . . . . . . . . . . . . . . . . . . . .203

100PF Services Appendix . . . . . . . . . . . . . . . . . .215

Wholesaling Appendix . . . . . . . . . . . . . . . . . . . .217

Glossary . . . . . . . . . . . . . . . . . . . . . . . . . . . . . . .227

Index . . . . . . . . . . . . . . . . . . . . . . . . . . . . . . . . .245

# DOWNLOAD THE FREE PROPERTY DEAL ANALYZER TOOL AND OTHER GREAT RESOURCES TODAY!

I've discovered that readers have the most favorable outcome when they use the Property Deal Analyzer Tool while reading my book.

As a big *Thank You* for purchasing the book, I'd like to give you the *Property Deal Analyzer Tool*, the Workbook: *How to Analyze a Deal*, and plenty other great resources 100% free!

**DOWNLOAD FREE INSTANTLY HERE**

http://www.100percentfinanced.com/content-hub

# Introduction

Many of you are reading this book for various freedom reasons. You want financial freedom. You think you want to get into real estate. You may even want to simply develop passive income. No matter the reason why you chose to pick up this book, it can all be summed up in one word: frustrated. You're frustrated with your 9-to-5. You're frustrated working 40 plus hours a week at a job that is unfulfilling.

You have no control over your time or earning potential. When I landed my first job after college, I felt the same way . I was frustrated that I had to ask "permission" to take a day off, take a lunch break, or take a vacation. While I was smart enough to finish an eight-hour day's worth of work in five hours, I was forced to remain at my desk until it was time for me to clock out. I was tired of being a broke frustrated chump living paycheck to paycheck.

Although I complained frequently, I did little to change my situation—until I was forced to change.

While I delegated tasks to others in my supervisory position with the federal government, inwardly I was searching for more. I knew I had greater, untapped potential.

I remember one time of starting a friendly contest in the office to increase employee engagement. I wanted to be the best at what I did so I created the contest to improve results. I've always been very competitive and wanted to achieve better outcomes.

After outlining the specifics of the contest, many of my team members achieved outstanding results. Many of them only wanted to win the contest for bragging rights. Our surveys usually only achieved a response rate of 25%, but as a result of the contest, we completed the first week at 65%!

The following day, my supervisor called me into her office. With my head held high and shoulders back I headed towards her office. Despite my proud Kool-Aid smile, she sternly suggested I have a seat. I sat down as she leaned over her desk with a scowl.

"Juan Pablo, what do you think you are doing?"

"Ummm, getting results," I said, laughingly. Unfortunately, she didn't find it funny. It actually fueled her anger.

"Don't you know you work for the government? There are policies, procedures, red tape and bureaucracy that you have to follow! You just can't *incentivize* your staff with monetary value to get results."

Confused, I asked, "But you treat us out to drinks every time we achieve great results. So aren't you incentivizing us with monetary value, too?" I could see her blood boiling.

"But I don't send out a mass email advertising it! You know what, Juan Pablo? Maybe the government isn't for you. Perhaps you are better suited for the private sector. As a result of this contest, I'm placing a written warning in your folder. Do not do anything like this again. You may leave my office now."

I left her office thinking, *"I obtained great results for thinking outside the box; but instead of being congratulated, I was reprimanded."* But something she said struck a chord with me. It was the greatest advice I ever received. Maybe the government wasn't for me. Perhaps I'd be better suited working for myself. That confrontation was the straw that broke the camel's back. I had a chip on my shoulder. I was no longer going to be that person who complained without making any changes. I decided I would no longer be a broke frustrated chump.

I walked back to my desk and immediately typed my resignation letter. I didn't physically resign that day, but I did in my mind. I decided to use that same "out of the box" thinking and apply it to real estate investing. I firmly decided to quit my day job at 30 years old.

I post-dated my resignation letter for my 30th birthday to embark on real estate investing. At the time, I was 26 years old with bad credit, no money, and no real estate investing experience; but, I had time. After reading a couple books about real estate investing, I used my spare time to acquire wealth.

Immediately, I started networking. I talked about real estate investing with everyone I encountered. I hoped to connect with someone who was an active real estate investor. I knew that in order to be successful, I had to surround myself with people who were already at the place I was trying to go.

One day after church service, I met Joko. After discovering that he was an aspiring businessman who read similar books, we became friends. He later told me about a real estate investing group he heard about in Harlem, which met once a month. When I logged onto the website, I noticed there were 600 registered members. I signed up immediately. I arrived thirty minutes before the meeting, and to my surprise, I was the only new member!

Out of 600 members, I thought there would be a slew of new people. As the only new member, I was able to have one-on-one time with my new mentor. Meeting Duane for the first time was exciting, but he didn't look like a real estate investor. I thought a real estate investor had to be suited and booted, looking as sharp as a thumbtack. He wore a hoodie, some loose fitting jeans, and some well-worn Adidas.

Duane immediately shared the size of his portfolio, as well as information about the many businesses he owned. He was a serial entrepreneur. With a big smile, he asked, "So, what brings you here?"

I was there because I was frustrated with working at a job that sucked. I wanted to learn real estate investing so I could quit. I didn't give Duane the whole truth though. "Well, I think it'll be cool to own a property or two." I did not feel comfortable sharing my true desires with him. Since I was meeting him for the first time, I didn't want him to think my hopes were far-fetched.

Duane could tell I was hiding something. He looked me in my eyes, poked my chest with his finger, and yelled in a stern voice, "My goal for you is to say goodbye to the 9-to-5!"

I was floored; I was shocked to learn that someone else had a significant goal for me that did not align with societal norms. Society teaches us to go to school, get a job, and retire. But, Duane was pushing me to pursue my burning desire, despite what society thinks. At that moment, my desire to quit my day job within four years became solidified and confirmed. I didn't know how I was going to do it, but I knew I needed to get started down the road to my financial freedom.

##  KEY PRINCIPLES

- **Stop complaining.** If your day job makes you frustrated, don't complain and do nothing. Use that frustration to make a positive change.

- **Networking is key.** I networked and read books in my spare time. Use your spare time to network to make your future self wealthy.

- **Find a mentor.** Find someone who is already doing what you aspire to do, and ask them to mentor you. Birds of a feather truly do flock together.

- **Qualify your mentors.** Don't just take advice from anyone. Check his or her success track record.

I, for one, would make a great mentor for you; because at the time of this writing, I have 63 rental units in my portfolio. I own a property management business, and an online business that teaches financial freedom while providing financial services through 100 Percent Financed (100PF). I became a licensed real estate agent and mortgage broker because I wanted to learn the ins and outs of the real estate industry and market. I'm also a public speaker and self-published author. I have been financially free since age 30, when I quit my day job. I am here to teach you how you, too, can quit your day job.

# Road to Financial Freedom

## *Convert Dreams Into Goals*

In 2009, I was renting a room for $850 per month in Jersey City, New Jersey, not too far from my job in New York City. I had a burning desire to invest in real estate, even though I didn't know how to get started. My landlord, Rose, was a homestay host for international students. Since she was much older than the students and had other things to focus on, I took it upon myself to welcome the students into her home, clean the bedrooms, take out the trash, and guide the students on tours throughout NYC. Rose was so impressed, she eventually presented me with a proposition.

"Juan, the summertime is approaching. If you give up your bedroom and sleep on my living room floor, I will allow you to stay here for free during the summer—as long as you can continue to help me like you're helping me now."

Rose knew summertime was a busy time for the homestay business. She also knew she could get more money for my room since the room rates always increased in the summer. I was interested in saving money, so I gave up my bed to an international student. At the end of that summer, I'd saved $3,000, which was the most money I'd saved in my entire life!

One day, as Rose and I strolled the streets of Jersey City, I noticed several duplexes and triplexes with "For Rent" signs. I wrote down the addresses and contact numbers on an old receipt I had in my pocket.

Normally, I spent thirty minutes of every lunch hour working on activities that could potentially improve my financial situation. So the next day, I took that receipt and called all ten-phone numbers listed. The tenth contact said she had a three-bedroom basement apartment, utilities included in the rent for $850 per month.

I thought, *"Wait a minute. Before Rose allowed me to stay at her house for free, I was paying her $850 a month for a furnished bedroom including utilities."* Now, I'd found an unfurnished *three-bedroom* apartment, including utilities, for the same amount.

I took a look at the apartment that evening, which was only one block away from Rose's house. The basement apartment was far from glamorous. It was damp and it had mold. The carpet smelled horribly; it had low ceilings and a rodent problem. In addition, one of the bedrooms was accessible only by walking through the other bedroom. Even still, it smelled like money to me! I told Rose about the opportunity and asked for her advice. She advised me to contact the three international student agencies she worked for so I could get multiple contracts in place for me to host students. I could host students for $700 per month, per room. She also advised me to clean the carpet, paint the walls, hire an exterminator, and furnish the place via The Salvation Army and thrift stores.

I contacted the landlord of the basement apartment to inform her that I wanted to rent it. While the lease forbade me from subleasing, I explained upfront that part of my job included subleasing. I told her about hosting international students from around the world and explained that she would see many faces of all races. However, I reassured her that I would be the master tenant. She agreed to revise the lease allowing me to sublease. I poured all of my $3,000 savings into the first month's rent, last month's rent, cleaning, painting and buying furniture. Considering that mold and rodent removal was the owner's responsibility, I went ahead and bit the bullet and paid for these services to rectify the situation, so that the international students could immediately move into a rent-ready apartment.

With just a $3,000 investment, I rented all three bedrooms to the international students while I slept on a futon in the living room. That was a huge upgrade for me. No longer was I renting a room; I was renting an entire apartment. No longer was I sleeping on the living room floor; I now slept on the futon. I received $2,100 in rent from three international students every month, but I was only paying the new landlord $850 per month in rent. After expenses and taxes, I was cash flowing approximately $1,000 per month.

> Cash flow is the profit you receive from your rental property after all operating expenses, reserves, and debt service is paid. It's the passive income for real estate. Control is better than ownership.
> –John D. Rockerfeller

I was making money off a property—a beat up, ugly property—that I did not own. This was my first investment. In hindsight, I realized I did a pseudo-lease option. As I cash flowed $1,000 per month, I dreamed of owning my first investment property; however, I still didn't know how to get started.

Naturally, I searched online for information on how to get started in real estate investing. You may have done the same thing. If you were to go to YouTube and browse videos of individuals who look successful (i.e. nice car, nice house, a fat check in his/her hand, surrounded by beautiful people, etc.), and after watching a few videos, you'll realize this person participated in wholesale real estate, flipping real estate, stock trading or has an online business to obtain results. Most people see the results and copy the exact route that the youtuber has taken. However, that's not quite the path to financial freedom. The people in the videos may have different starting points than you, which can lead you to take a different route.

For example, before you embark on a road trip, you program your GPS. The GPS requires you to enter the address of your final destination, and then it presents you with several routes. The quickest route may be expensive, because it may require paying tolls that will cost you more in the long run. The less expensive route may not contain any tolls, but it will take you longer to arrive at your final destination. You must also factor in the vehicle you're driving. Consider taking a van if you need to accommodate a lot of people along the journey. If you want to arrive quickly, consider driving a Ferrari. After considering all these factors, soon you'll realize that your route may be different from others.

You have to rearrange some things! First, you must calculate where you're starting out financially. Then, you have to determine your final destination. What does financial freedom mean to you specifically? Then, calculate the best route for you to take based upon your market, your investment vehicle, as well as your tolerance for risk.

The problem is that you may have dreams, but keep them just that—dreams. Dreams are for kids! Goals are for adults. Don't get me wrong; dreams are good because they make us feel good. However, we must convert those dreams into goals if we ever want to accomplish them.

When you make your dreams specific, quantifiable, measurable and actionable, and set solid deadlines, you have converted them into tangible goals. Turn your dream of becoming financially free into a goal.

 *Let's get started by calculating your starting point.*

1. **Calculate your debt-to-income (DTI) ratio.** To determine your DTI ratio, simply take your total amount of debt and divide it by your income. For instance, if your debt is $3,000 per month, and your monthly income equals $5,000, your DTI is $3,000 ÷ $5,000, or 60%. Write this ratio onto the worksheet provided. Aim for a DTI of 40% or lower to qualify for most mortgages. You can improve this ratio by paying down debt or increasing your monthly income.

2. **Order a copy of your credit report.** Use annualcreditreport.com to obtain a free credit report. You can only order this report once a year. I recommend using identityiq.com (www.identityiq.com/help-you-to-save-money.aspx?offercode=431134LD) so you can monitor your credit on a monthly basis. Notate your FICO score for all three bureaus, your debt-to-credit (DTC) ratio, and the number of hard inquiries you have on all three credit bureaus on the worksheet below. If your credit monitoring service doesn't provide you with your DTC ratio, you'll have to calculate it yourself. To determine

your DTC ratio, simply take the amount of debt you have charged to that revolving account and divide it by your maximum limit. For instance, if your credit card has a balance of $7,000, and the maximum limit for that credit card account is $10,000, then your DTC is $7,000 ÷ $10,000, or 70%. Write this ratio at the bottom now. Aim for a DTC of 30% or lower to qualify for most mortgages and business credit. You can improve your DTC ratio by requesting credit line increases on all of your revolving credit card accounts and by paying down debt.

3. **Calculate your net worth.** Net worth is defined as assets minus liabilities. For instance, let's say you own the house you live in, as well as a car. Upon research, you discovered that your home appraised at $100,000, and your car has a value of $20,000. Then, you check with your lender to find out you owe $65,000 on your mortgage and $12,000 on your car note. In this instance, you would have a net worth of ($100,000 + $20,000) - ($65,000 + $12,000) = $43,000. Net worth is important; you can use it as leverage for real estate investing. Moreover, mortgage lenders feel comfortable lending a certain mortgage amount when it is somewhat equal to the borrower's net worth. In other

words, they want to make sure you're suable. If you do not have a substantial net worth that matches the mortgage amount you need, it's okay. Again, we're calculating your starting point so we can create a path to financial freedom. That is what strategic partnerships are for. For this exercise, please write your net worth on the worksheet. Real estate investing requires your time. It requires your undivided attention and uninterrupted focused hours. If you are serious about financial freedom, you need to be an excellent steward of your time. Write down how many hours a week you can devote toward real estate related activities (reading, attending seminars, networking, cold-calling brokers and analyzing deals). I recommend carving out 20 hours a week to make yourself wealthy.

4. **Capital.** How much capital do you have access to for real estate investing? Calculate the total amount of cash you can liquidate including savings, retirement accounts, business credit, pulling out cash from a car you own free and clear, and pulling out equity from a property you own. Add the total amount to the worksheet. This money will cover the down payment, soft costs and closing costs. These values refer to your total out-of-pocket cash. To calculate how big of a deal

you can close, take your capital and divide it by .20. Then, divide it by $30,000. If you have access to $40,000, and structure a deal in which the seller is providing a 10% note for seller financing, divide $40,000/.2. This shows that you can afford a $200,000 purchase price. Divide $200,000 by $30,000 per door, which equals 6.67 units. If you were investing in a market in which the cost per unit was $30,000, and you had $40,000 in cash and negotiated 10% seller financing, you could afford to buy a six-unit apartment building (assuming there are units like this in your market). If you do not have access to cash, you need to partner with someone who will bring the total out-of-pocket cash to the table. Aim for roughly $40,000 per deal.

5. **Monthly Living Expenses.** The following Starting Point Worksheet is a snapshot of your financial dashboard, created so that you can find out where you currently stand financially. For section one of the worksheet, A through G, you only need to know where you are and where you want to end. I would like you to compare it to the metrics below so that you'll have something to aim for.

In order to wrap up your financial dashboard, you need to calculate your monthly living expenses beginning with how much you pay for housing, utilities, transportation, credit cards, loans, food, clothing, entertainment and anything else you can think of. Write these numbers in section two of the worksheet, H through L, and add these numbers up to get your total monthly living expenses. Most people don't know their monthly living expenses; thus, I would like to clarify a few things to make sure you factor everything correctly.

a. Your Debt-to-Income Ratio should be 40% or lower.

b. Aim for a FICO Score of 680 or higher.

c. Your Debt-to-Credit Ratio should be 30% or lower.

d. No more than 5 inquiries within the past 6 months.

e. Your Net Worth needs to be equal to or greater than the amount of money you intend to borrow from a mortgage company.

f. The Number of Hours per Week spent on Real Estate should be 20 at minimum.

g. The Capital You Have Access to ideally should be $20,000 or more.

h. Calculate your monthly mortgage (PITI) or rent amount. If you pay Homeowners Association fees, include that in your calculation.

i. If you own or lease a car, make sure you factor in car insurance, gas, maintenance, permits, licenses, parking, tolls along with any other expenses that apply to the vehicle. If you use public transportation, include your total monthly expenses.

j. Calculate your minimum monthly payment on all revolving debt, such as credit card debt. Revolving debt is defined as debt in which you can charge, pay down, and charge again. Again, only add the monthly minimum payment for all revolving debt.

k. Calculate your monthly minimum payment on all installment debt (student loans, car loans, etc.). Installment debt allows you to make fixed payments over a fixed period of time. Once the loan is paid in full, you are unable to charge anything else. Again, only add the minimum monthly payment for all installment debt.

1. Calculate the monthly amount you're currently saving. If you are not currently saving anything, write in $500. If you find yourself living paycheck to paycheck, look for ways to reduce your current living expenses short-term while you're working on obtaining passive income via real estate investing. If you spend $1,000 a month on dining out, reduce it to $500 a month. If you have cable, cut it off! Again, you're making short-term sacrifices to reach your financial destination at a much faster pace. Yes, you deserve the new outfit, the new car, the latest phone, and even your favorite glass of wine since you work so hard. However, that is the reason so few people are financially free. "Entrepreneurs do what most people won't do in the beginning to later be able to do what most people can't do." If you make these short-term sacrifices in your spending habits, you'll later be in a position to do things that most people only dream of doing. If you need additional assistance calculating your personal living expenses, subscribe to www.100percentfinanced.com and download the free Personal Financial Statement. Your target goal is to save at least $500 per month.

In "Other," include other monthly expenses not included below (child support, gym memberships, online memberships, etc.). Write the total amount below.

Double check your work. Confirm these totals with your significant other to make sure you're not leaving out any expenses. Add up your monthly living expenses, and write the total amount on the next page.

# STARTING POINT

| | | GOAL |
|---|---|---|
| Debt-to-Income Ratio: | _____ | 40% or ↓ |
| FICO Score: *(Experian, Equifax, TransUnion)* | _____ | 680 |
| Debt-to-Credit Ratio: | _____ | 30% or ↓ |
| Inquiries: | _____ | 5 or ↓ |
| Net Worth: | _____ | $50,000+ |
| Number of Hours per Week: | _____ | 20 HOURS |
| Capital You Have Access to: | _____ | $20,000 |

Housing: _____

Utilities, Cable, Internet, Phone: _____

Transportation: _____

Credit Cards: _____

Loans (Student, Other): _____

Savings: _____

Food: _____

Clothing: _____

Entertainment: _____

Other: _____

**Total Monthly Living Expenses:** _____

Now, it's time to do the fun part! We will now calculate your financial destination. You will now calculate how much passive income you need on a monthly basis to quit your job, as well as how many units you need in your portfolio before you can resign from your 9-to-5.

1. **PILE Formula.** PILE is an acronym for **P**assive **I**ncome > **L**iving **E**xpenses. Ideally, you want your passive income to exceed your personal living expenses by 150%. You add this 150% buffer to account for the expenses you forgot to calculate in your monthly living expenses. The average person doesn't budget for haircuts, buying Christmas and birthday gifts, oil changes, paying your tax guy and other small charges that add up over time. The 150% (or multiplying your monthly living expenses by 1.5) is a buffer to account for those missing items. Once you calculate the math below, you've now discovered your financial freedom goal. If my monthly living expenses amounted to $5,000 a month, and I multiplied it by 1.5, I would yield a financial freedom goal of $7,500 a month. The financial freedom goal equals the amount of passive income needed each month to turn in your resignation letter to that job that sucks. Do the math in the chart below.

2. **Units.** Now that you know what your financial freedom goal is, it's time to see how many units you need in your portfolio to generate your financial freedom goal. On average, you should profit (cash flow) $100 to $150 per rental unit. So, if you have a ten-unit apartment building, you should aim to cash flow 10 units times $150 per unit, which equals $1,500 a month; however, be willing to settle for $1000. Now, divide your financial freedom goal by $150. This amount lets you know how many units you should aim to hold in your portfolio. In the above scenario, if my financial freedom goal was $7,500, and I divide it by $150 per unit, I should aim to acquire 50 rental units. Enter your total unit goal on the Financial Destination worksheet.

3. **Financial freedom.** If you don't have a ton of savings or stellar credit, but you do have the self-discipline to work on real estate in your part-time for at least 20 hours a week, and if you follow the steps outlined, you will be able to quit your day job in five years maximum of picking up this book. Now, it is possible to quit your day job in two years if you are extremely aggressive; however, I prefer a five year plan. Divide your Total Unit Goal by five years to calculate your Yearly Unit Goal. Now, you're breaking down

your goals even further. When you divide 50 units by five years, you know you need to acquire 10 rental units a year, minimum. This acquisition can happen in many ways. You can buy a ten-unit apartment building every year for the next five years, or a six-unit and a four-unit (just two closings a year). Your primary focus is the amount of cash flow you will be receiving, not necessarily the number of units and return on investment.

If you need $7,500 a month in passive income, you can obtain this goal by acquiring $1,500 in cash flow per year. If your market has single-family homes with the average cash flow of $250 per unit, this may equate to you having to close on six single-family homes a year for the next five years. If you close six single families a year (adding $1,500 cash flow per year in your portfolio for the next five years), you'll only need to have 30 units in your portfolio, not 50.

You have to be flexible based upon your market. I'd suggest buying a multi-unit property since buying one ten-unit or a 10-unit portfolio a year will be less burdensome that purchasing six separate single-family homes a year.

Remember, I started off broke with bad credit. Today, I own 63 rental units. I'll teach you how to do the same. Just have faith, and write your Yearly Unit Goal below. Keep in mind, you can buy 10-single family homes in one single transaction in a portfolio, this will help you become financially free as fast as buying 10-units all under one roof. Don't turn your nose up at portfolios, single-family, or cash-flowing units less than $100 a door; be adaptable to the market.

So far, you've calculated your starting point as well as your financial destination. Now you know how much passive income you need and how many units you need in your portfolio. You've successfully converted your dream of financial freedom into a goal. Pat yourself on the back. If you are reading this and did not complete the previous charts, go back and do so. Do not move forward without completing the charts. Do not be one of those people who read, accumulate knowledge, but fail to put it into action.

Every deal is different. Every market is different. Every financial instrument is different. In February of 2014, I closed on a nine-unit apartment building. It generated a cash flow of $800 a month ($9600 a year). The cash flow for this nine-unit apartment building is $88.89 per unit! I got it 100% financed. I obtained this income-producing asset using little

# FINANCIAL DESTINATION

PILE: Total Expenses x 1.5 _____

Total Units Goal: PILE / $150/unit _____

Yearly Unit Goal: TUG / 5 years _____

*My Goal for You*

to none of my own money. Because I used 100% financing, the debt service was higher, resulting in smaller cash flow. However, I didn't care. That's an additional $800 of passive income per month that I did not have before.

In this instance, if my financial freedom goal was $7,500 per month, I would subtract $800 from the $7,500 to derive at a total of $6,700 per month in passive income. This would be the amount required to quit my day job. Sure, I may have to acquire additional units as a result of the cash flow per unit amount being less, but that's fine.

After closing every deal, be sure to subtract the cash flow from the financial freedom goal until you get to $0. Once you get to a financial freedom goal of $0, turn in your two weeks' notice to your boss immediately. At 100PF, our goal is to have 100,000 early retirees as a result of our teachings and seminars. Once you become financially free, please email us at info@100percentfinanced.com and let us know you became financially free as a result of our teachings and/or services.

# PERSONAL BILLBOARDS FOR SUCCESS

Now that you've calculated your starting point and financial destination, it's time to start your engines! As you embark on this journey, you will need "billboards" in sight.

I love road trips, and I love Chick-fil-A. One time, my old friend Ryan and I were driving from Atlanta, Georgia to New York City to host an event. During our drive, I saw a Chick-fil-A billboard. I suggested pulling over to get some food, but Ryan insisted on driving until we got to a quarter tank of gas remaining. That way, we could fill up the tank and our stomachs in one stop. Nevertheless, every ten to fifteen miles, I kept seeing this same billboard. I couldn't take it any longer. I told Ryan to pull over at the next exit to grab something to eat from Chick-fil-A.

Billboards, along with other advertisements, are vital. If you have watched a 100PF YouTube video, you've seen the ads. If you have watched the Super Bowl, you've seen the ads. If you have ever visited Times Square in New York City, you've seen the ads. Companies are willing to spend millions of dollars on ads because they know that if you see an image repeatedly, more than likely, you will take action towards obtaining it.

So, why not create your personal billboards for success? If you place your personal billboards where you can see them repeatedly, they will eventually cause you to make moves toward obtaining your goals.

The creed and resignation letter are your personal billboards for success. Fill in the creed and resignation letter on the following pages and place them on your bedroom door. Tear the following pages out, tape it to your door, and read it aloud daily. Also, visualize yourself completing the tasks outlined in your personal billboards for success.

# *Creed*

If I, _____, do not close on my first
　　　*(Write your name above)*
multifamily property by December 31, _____,
　　　　　　　　　　　　　　　　　　　　　　*(Write in next year)*
I deserve to remain in my current financial situation.

Nevertheless, I will obtain this goal because I have every resource at my disposal to make this a reality.

_____
Signature

# *Resignation Letter*

Dear _____,
*(Enter employer's name)*

This letter is to my express my gratitude for being hired with this company. I have gained a wealth of knowledge and experience while working here.

However, it has been difficult for me to pursue my passion while being constrained to a "9-to-5."

Therefore, I choose to retire at the ripe age of \_\_\_\_\_
*(Enter your age five years from today)*
because I have successfully acquired many assets to afford my lifestyle.

I bid you a bittersweet farewell. I hope that you will find a well-qualified replacement who will be thrilled to occupy my position.

_____
Signature

_____
*(Enter today's date five years from today)*

Michael, from New England, someone I once mentored, wrote his creed in late 2015. With the help of business credit and a partner, he closed on his first cash flowing investment property—a triplex! Being that the creed was at the forefront of his mind day in and day out, purchasing his first investment property by December 2016 was Michael's most dominant thought. He found ways to make his intention a reality. Make sure you write your creed. Keep an open mind, and think of ways to close on your first deal, like Michael. He eventually scratched out "first investment property" and wrote "second investment property" directly above it. He will definitely find his next deal.

So after I moved into the new apartment and completed the Starting Point checklist, the Financial Destination sheet, and the Personal Billboards for Success letters, I had such a burning desire to succeed. No longer was I scared of taking action towards buying a property. As I embarked on this journey to financial freedom, I ran into my first roadblock: I got a flat tire. I had bad credit, which needed dire repair. Plus, I didn't know the best route to take to buy my first investment property.

*If you need an improved FICO score, 100PF is here to help.*

In the next chapter, you will learn how you can overcome this obstacle that's hindering you from reaching your financial destination.

 ## KEY PRINCIPLES

- **Ignorance is not bliss, but knowing is.** Know your financials so you can improve them.

- **Sweep your own porch.** You must sweep your own porch before you sweep someone else's. You must manage your personal numbers before you can do the same for business. If you don't know your own personal finances (credit score, net worth, etc.), how can you analyze the financials of a multifamily apartment building?

- **Create a burning desire.** Your personal billboards for success will create a burning desire within you to get over the things that hold you back, like fear and laziness.

- **Maintain the right mindset.** Every deal, every market, and every financial instrument are different. Nevertheless, you have the potential to make money in every market as long as you maintain the right mindset.

- **Everything can be fixed.** If your debt-to-credit ratio is too high, credit score and savings are too low, don't worry. You can fix all of them in time.

- **Don't be a copycat.** Don't just "copy and paste" someone else's route without first knowing how they got started. You may have to create your own unique route.

- **Make SMART goals.** If your dreams aren't quantifiable, measurable, specific and actionable, and if you don't have a deadline associated with them, you are living a fantasy.

- **Do not be lazy.** You may not be a numbers person. You may even have a hard time coming up with the numbers. Make sure you get it done before advancing to the next chapter. Again, if you cannot manage your personal numbers, how can you manage the numbers of any business?

- **Search for rental units.** In the above scenario about the ten-unit cash flowing at $1,500 a month, what if you find a ten-unit apartment building in which the total cash flow was $800 ($80/unit), requiring none of your own money in the deal (100% financed)? Would you turn this deal down, assuming there were no other deals on the table? I would hope not! Even though it's not cash flowing $150/unit, there is still an additional $800 cash flow per month in your portfolio, $9,600 a year, that you did not have previously! It's still a plus. You simply may have to look for more rental units. Continue to update your personal financial statement reflecting this new cash flow.

- **Find a mentor.** Rose was my mentor. She showed me the ropes and she had an abundance mindset. There are people out there who wouldn't mind helping you; but you must first help them. Remember, I offered to help Rose with her students first. Then, she later helped me obtain my own students. She didn't consider me as her competition because of the abundance of students, opportunities, and money available in our market.

- **Control is better than ownership.** You can make money off assets that you do not own.

- **Evaluate all consequences up front.** Before I signed the lease with the new landlord, I requested that she remove the "unable to sublease" language out of the lease instead of subleasing it behind her back. I also signed contracts with the international agencies and knew how much it would cost to clean, fix, and furnish the apartment before I signed the lease with the new landlord. I knew all of my numbers up front.

- **Reinvest your earnings.** I saved $3,000, and then reinvested it into an asset I did not own. I ultimately cash flowed $1,000 a month and reinvested it to make my credit better. I also saved for a down payment. Reinvestment is easy to do when you have your eyes on the prize—and keep them there.

# FIRST ROADBLOCK:
# Fixing Bad Credit

I desperately wanted to purchase my first investment property; however, I didn't qualify for mortgages. I couldn't obtain funding via business credit because my personal credit was bad. My credit score was in the 500s. Collection companies called me daily, sometimes all day long. I was scared to pick up the phone from an unrecognizable phone number. My FICO score was holding me back for business and personal reasons.

In an effort to achieve financial freedom, it's important to know how the FICO score is calculated before you proceed with making it pretty.

## CALCULATION OF THE FICO SCORE:

35% - Payment History

30% - Debt-to-Credit Ratio

15% - Length of Credit History

10% - Types of Credit

10% - Number of Credit Inquiries

At that time, my debt-to-credit ratio was too high. I had a bad payment history and a large number of hard inquiries from applying for financing. I even closed some of my department store credit cards because I did not use them.

Credit is important. Your credit represents your credibility or reputation to banks (the guys who lend you money). Having "good credit" can help you obtain both personal and business loans. Most startups and beginner real estate investors want to secure funding in their business name without having to personally guarantee anything. However, seeing that your business is brand new, most lenders will look at your personal credit.

Banks are smart. They make millions of dollars by lending money. They understand that it's risky to lend money to new businesses that do not have Profit & Loss statements (P & Ls), bank statements, or tax returns. Imagine that your business is your baby; it's new and inexperienced. If your baby tries to get a loan based on her credibility, the bank will decline the loan. The banks may consider lending the money to the baby if the parent is credible enough financially to handle the loan. Lenders look at the business owner's (parent) credit report and other financials. If the business owner is credible, financially speaking, the bank will extend the loan to the business with a personal guarantee.

Bankers also think, "If this new business owner is prudent in managing his or her personal finances (hence the high FICO score), the new business owner will be prudent in managing a business' finances". Thus, they agree to the loan with a personal guarantee. Sure, you can obtain funding for a business without a personal guarantee, but you have to make sure your business is not a baby. It must be in compliance with state and federal laws, have a paydex score of 80 and tax returns, Profit and Loss Statement, merchant account statements, and bank statements from past years. The qualifications below will not only get you approved for business credit that can help you with down payment assistance, we'll discuss this later, but these will also improve your credit score significantly:

1. Average FICO score from all three credit bureaus: 720 or higher.

2. DTC: 30% or lower.

3. Inquiries: Fewer than five per credit bureau.

4. No bankruptcies, foreclosures, or other judgments.

5. No late payments in the past 24 months.

6. One major credit card with a maximum limit of $5,000.

7. A ten-year credit history.

Also, apply for business credit as an additional source of funding to assist you with the down payment on your multi-unit rentals. New businesses can receive up to $75,000 in financing, but seasoned businesses (businesses incorporated longer than two years) can receive up to $150,000. Even if you do not meet the standard qualifications, apply anyway. Apply for business credit at www.100percentfinanced.com. We can create a plan for you to get qualified in the future. There are no upfront fees; this is simply a free consultation. If your credit isn't where you want it to be right now, that's okay. You can always improve it. One way to do this is through credit repair.

Regardless of what people may think, credit repair is perfectly legal. Credit repair is when you request a creditor to prove that an account listed in your credit file is reporting accurate and verifiable information. If a creditor or credit bureau is unable to provide the requested documentation, by law, they are required to remove any inaccurate information from your report. If an item/account cannot be proven, it does not exist.

You can dispute the following negative items on your credit report:

✗ Late payments on closed accounts

✗ Collection accounts

✗ Charge-offs, medical bills and evictions

✗ Judgments, repossessions and foreclosures

✗ Discharged bankruptcies

✗ Tax liens

We can provide credit repair services for you, or you can do it yourself. Visit 100percentfinanced.com to learn more. However, before we jump into the next chapter, there are a few more things I want to share about how to fix your credit.

You can also improve your credit by doing the following:

1. Request credit line increases every six months without the creditor doing a hard pull on your credit, for this causes a hard inquiry and can potentially lower your FICO score.

2. Pay down debt on revolving credit cards.

3. Keep accounts open even if you do not use them (i.e. department store credit cards).

4. Dispute closed derogatory items (collection accounts, judgments, bankruptcies, tax liens, medical bills, evictions), as well as hard inquiries from where you did not receive personal accounts.

Visit www.100percentfinanced.com for additional information.

We've had a countless number of credit repair clients who have achieved excellent results. Many of them were able to apply for a mortgage, business credit, or an auto loan after successfully completing our program. Of course, you can invest in real estate without perfect credit. Nevertheless, having a great credit score makes the deal much more profitable for you.

In 2010, I disputed negative items on my credit report, paid down some debt, and requested credit line increases. Once my credit was fixed, and after I recited the creed and visualized handing in my resignation letter, I was able to qualify for an FHA mortgage for a duplex! I was able to live in one unit and rent out the other. My first property was both a personal residence and an investment property. The date on my creed was December 31, 2010; however, I closed on my first property on March 31, 2010. I was on my way to financial freedom!

At first, I was shocked that the creed actually worked. I went back to the creed and scratched out "First Investment Property" and then wrote directly above it, "Second Investment Property." I closed on my second property on December 7, 2010! The creed worked! I bought my second investment property out of state by using the lump sum I received from an auto refinance I did through my credit union, as well as receiving cash advances from my personal credit cards. I found out later that using personal credit cards for real estate investing is not a wise decision. For one reason, the interest rate on a credit card is normally four times higher than the appreciation rate of the property. Also, it raises your debt-to-credit ratio and debt-to-income ratio preventing you from qualifying for financing in the future. However, I was cash flowing! By the end of 2010, I owned three units.

In 2011, I didn't purchase any properties. I was still getting acclimated to property management. I needed to figure out how to have proper work/business management, and I was saving aggressively for my next deal. It was a tough year. I had to fire two property management companies:

1. The tenant wasn't paying the water bill; he just paid the rent. In Pennsylvania, the water company can place a lien on the property if the water bill is not paid, but the property manager did not care. I told him I wanted the tenant evicted and he decided to heed my request 17 days later. I fired the property manager as soon as the tenant was evicted.

2. I hired another property manager and didn't realize that I needed to pay his commission, even if the unit was vacant. I blame myself for signing a contract without fully reading or having it reviewed by an attorney. But, this was a blessing in disguise because I figured out how to manage properties out of state, which lead to me forming my own property management company. In 2011, my real estate investing endeavors fell flat; however, I made it through. In 2012, my finances

improved; however, I was nowhere close to the financial goals I set in order to quit my job the following year. My credit was much better, but after spending months saving thousands of dollars, I realized I was running out of cash. I was running out of gas on this road to financial freedom. I realized that I needed a consistent source of funds, so I would never run out of gas on my road to financial freedom again.

 **KEY PRINCIPLES**

- **Work with qualified professionals.** Have your attorney review documents you don't understand.

- **Screen your team properly.** Ask for references.

- **Don't just sit there; do something!** If you realize something is holding you back, do something about it. Get your credit fixed!

- **Get your credit report.** Order your credit report if you have not done so already. Dispute all negative items.

- **Don't answer the phone.** If collection companies keep calling you, you do not have to answer. Dispute the account. After several disputes, consider settling the account for 50 cents on the dollar or less, as long as they agree in writing to remove the collection account from your credit report.

- **Keep your eyes on the prize.** If you continue to look at your personal billboards of success, you will achieve your goals. Don't worry about the how; just focus on the why.

- **Be prudent.** If you're not prudent in managing your own finances, how can you be prudent in managing business finances?

- **Success doesn't have to be linear.** While you're studying real estate investing, attend networking events, get your credit repaired and have coffee with experienced real estate investors. Your network should increase your net worth!

# RUNNING OUT OF GAS:
# Feeling Burned Out

Today, you're an employee. You may spend one hour of your time commuting to work and an additional hour commuting back home. You may spend eight hours at your job. Plus, you may have other commitments, including family, friends, exercise, fantasy football, watching the housewives of some city on TV, attending church and more. Somewhere in there, you have to rest! You may feel like there's not enough hours in the day, and you lack energy. You may feel as if you're running out of gas.

This is where the rubber meets the road. I've coached countless number of students, and a small percentage of them never closed on a deal. They didn't have solid habits to make it happen; they were burnt out.

As an employee, you may be accustomed to having someone tell you what to do, how to do it, and when to do it. Your boss provides you with annual reviews, and the fear of getting fired or laid off is your prime motivation to do your job correctly. However, as a real estate entrepreneur, no one is going to look over your shoulder and inspect your work. No one will force you to perform your tasks a certain way, at a certain time. You have to keep yourself accountable. As an entrepreneur, you may not have an overseer. You probably enjoy leisure time and rest often because no one is holding you accountable. Without question, the book of *Proverbs* is my favorite book of the bible. Below are four passages from *Proverbs* that summarize the mindset of an entrepreneur.

Proverbs 6: 6-11 (KJV)

*6 Go to the ant, thou sluggard; consider her ways, and be wise:*

*7 Which having no guide, overseer, or ruler,*

*8 Provideth her meat in the summer, and gathereth her food in the harvest.*

*9 How long wilt thou sleep, O sluggard? when wilt thou arise out of thy sleep?*

*10 Yet a little sleep, a little slumber, a little folding of the hands to sleep:*

*11 So shall thy poverty come as one that travelleth, and thy want as an armed man.*

Proverbs 24:30-34 (KJV)

*30 I went by the field of the slothful, and by the vineyard of the man void of understanding;*

*31 And, lo, it was all grown over with thorns, and nettles had covered the face thereof, and the stone wall thereof was broken down.*

*32 Then I saw, and considered it well: I looked upon it, and received instruction.*

*33 Yet a little sleep, a little slumber, a little folding of the hands to sleep:*

*34 So shall thy poverty come as one that travelleth; and thy want as an armed man.*

Proverbs 26:13-16 (KJV)

*13 The slothful man saith, There is a lion in the way; a lion is in the streets.*

*14 As the door turneth upon his hinges, so doth the slothful upon his bed.*

*15 The slothful hideth his hand in his bosom; it grieveth him to bring it again to his mouth.*

*16 The sluggard is wiser in his own conceit than seven men that can render a reason.*

Proverbs 10:4 (KJV)

*4 He becometh poor that dealeth with a slack hand: but the hand of the diligent maketh rich.*

These proverbs discuss laziness, being your own boss, and working smart. They also define why most people are broke, why excuses prevent people from taking action, how lazy people start something, yet don't finish it (picking up a book and reading it, but don't place any of the author's advice into action), as well as how lazy people think they know it all and do things their own way.

It's clear how to get rich: by working smart and hard. Real estate investing is simple; however, it's not easy. It's not easy because it may be hard work for you to get out of bed early and apply the disciplines daily. You have to say, "No" to temptation; you have to master your time and become a good steward over your expenses. As you can see in the above proverb, *"Hard workers get rich."*

Real estate investing is similar to exercise. Many people desire to start working out around New Year's Day. They are frustrated with how they look and feel. They join a gym and implement an exercise regimen. If they have no personal trainer or accountability partner, there is no one to hold them accountable. Thus, when the workouts become difficult or conflict with their schedule, they don't show up at the gym. Soon, this becomes a habit.

They end up back at square one: a fat, frustrated chump who is physically unfit.

The same happens to you financially. You may be frustrated with your 9-to-5 because it sucks. You know you have untapped potential waiting to be expressed in your own business. As a result, you join a real estate networking event, purchase a book, or join an online real estate coaching program. But, since you don't have certain habits or an accountability partner, no one is there to hold you accountable. Thus, when the strategies you obtained become difficult or take up too much time of your day, you put the book down. This becomes a habit. Sooner or later, you're back at square one: a broke, frustrated chump who is financially unfit.

In this chapter we'll discuss carving out time, setting up your business, being self-disciplined and self-controlled enough to do the things you need to do.

You need energy in order to work full-time at your day job. The same is true for your real estate investing career. Your goal is to use your spare time wisely enough to make yourself wealthy. You may wake up at 7 a.m. daily. It may take you 30 minutes to shower, get dressed, eat breakfast, and head out the door to your day job. But, you hold the power to be more productive with your time if you follow a few daily morning disciplines.

Wake up an hour early. Place your alarm clock a significant distance away from your bed so you have to get out of bed to turn the alarm off. Don't hit the snooze button and crawl back into bed! You want financial freedom, right? Think about the signal you're sending to the world by hitting the snooze button. You're delaying discipline first thing in the morning. Start your day off right by adhering to this simple discipline. These disciplines will free you from your 9-to-5.

Upon waking, drink an eight-ounce glass of water. Do not eat anything until after you exercise for 30 minutes at home. Working out from home reduces the commute time you would waste going to the gym. In addition to random conversations at the gym, which serve as more of a distraction, you waste time changing clothes and waiting for someone to finish using the exercise machine you want to use. There are plenty of home workouts you can do. My favorite is *Beachbody on Demand*. I pay a monthly subscription for access to many workouts that concentrate on getting lean, building mass, and more. Personally, I prefer P90X3, since every workout is 30 minutes. Train your body to workout on an empty stomach. It may be difficult working out on an empty stomach first thing in the morning, but in time, you'll get used to it. Work out 30 minutes a day, for six days a week. Exercising first thing in the morning gets your blood pumping and eliminates any excuses concerning not having time to exercise based on the demands of the day. Make sure you drink another eight-ounce glass of water during your workout, as well as directly afterward. The more water, the better! Now, if your apartment is too small or you cannot afford a home workout, find simple workouts on YouTube or jog through your neighborhood. Find a way to get fit.

Read your affirmations for ten minutes daily and visualize yourself closing deals and living the financially free lifestyle. Read a real estate resource book for ten minutes daily, and be sure to take notes. Plan your real estate activities for the day. Take no more than five minutes for planning. Set an alarm for each real estate activity to notify you when it's time to switch to the next activity. For meetings with investors, other realtors, and attorneys, send them a Google calendar invite so you're both on the same page. Schedule everything! Leave nothing to the memory.

Ironing your clothes the day before is a time saver. During your commute, listen to an audiobook that will aid in your personal development. Sign up for an Audible.com account, if you don't already have one. Do not listen to the radio, music or the news. Use your commute time to listen to content that can potentially make you a better real estate investor and businessperson.

Get a Gmail and Google voice account. Link your Google voice number to your cell phone, as well as your direct work line (if you have one). Give the Google voice phone number to those in the real estate industry. This will be the best way for realtors, wholesalers, attorneys, contractors and tenants to contact you. When they call you, both your cell phone and direct office lines will ring simultaneously.

If you don't have a direct office line, answer your cell phone professionally. With Google voice, you can also type text messages from your computer. So, if someone from the real estate industry calls you, you can quickly text them back from your computer if your phone isn't accessible. Inform everyone on your real estate investing team of your "office hours." If you know you're normally free to talk around lunch or late afternoon, tell your team to call you around that time.

Devote 30 minutes of every lunch hour to real estate-related activities. Use this time to call your real estate team, to analyze deals, review listings, draft offers, search for mortgage brokers in your market and research market data. If possible, always eat your lunch at your desk. Eat two low carb meals a day, and pick one day out of the week to eat anything you want. Drink only water, tea and/or coffee (without copious amounts of creamer and sugar). Make sure these meals are whole foods, not processed. You need to have energy and alertness throughout the day, so don't eat heavy foods that will make you feel lethargic. Also, be sure to get out of the office, even if it's for a ten-minute walk to get some fresh air.

During office hours, be the workhorse, not the social butterfly. You may enjoy talking to your co-workers by the water cooler, or stopping by their cubicles to chat. But, keep in mind: you won't be working with these individuals for long. You're working two jobs: you're a full-time employee, as well as a part-time entrepreneur. You don't have the luxury for small talk. Stay focused; you don't have time to chit chat.

Avoid lengthy office meetings, if possible. The more time you stay near a computer and a phone, the more you'll be able to work on your real estate investing. It'll be difficult for you to reach out to your real estate team or analyze deals in a meeting. Explain to your supervisor that you have so much work to do that you must stay at your desk.

When you leave the office, listen to another audiobook or podcast. You can also devote this time to returning calls. If you're commuting via public transportation, and you don't have cell phone service, use this time to go over your affirmations or read a book.

When you reach home, spend one hour engulfed in real estate-related activities outlined in this book. This may involve reaching out to wholesalers, networking with partners, attending networking events, reviewing listings, consulting with your real estate attorney or looking at properties. If you have to look at properties, you can use this hour or use your lunch hour to do so. Make sure your time is undivided and focused.

You should attend at least two networking events a month, one of which should be real estate specific. Find local real estate groups or organizations, and join. Attend a different type of networking event once a month that will help you develop in both your business and personal life. Be intentional; schedule these events on your calendar.

Spend four hours on Saturday or Sunday networking, looking at listings on your computer, reading real estate-related material and/or attending seminars. If you apply the above disciplines daily, you'll soon notice that you have the time available to pursue your goal of becoming financially free. You just have to be disciplined. Dedicate at least 20 hours to your real estate investing endeavors in order to become financially free within two to five years. You'll have to treat real estate investing as a part- time job; use your spare time to make yourself wealthy. If you spend four hours on the weekend that leaves you with 16 hours during the week to make it happen. This equates to you working four hours a day Monday through Thursday, and four hours on Saturday. That allows you to have Friday and Sunday off! However, if you have the additional time, use it wisely.

I understand your schedule may not be a typical 9-to-5 shift. You may not have the space in your apartment to work out. Whatever the case may be, do your best to make it work. If you work part time at another job, you may consider quitting that job first and reducing your personal living expenses. Make sure you find the 20 hours to make it happen.

You have to really want financial freedom. If you have a burning desire, this will assist you in applying the disciplines. Don't go gung-ho in the beginning and run out of steam quickly. The first 30 days of application may be tough since you're forming a new habit. However, no one ever said something worth having comes easy. Getting in shape sounds great, but it may not be easy since you'll have to form new habits. You may feel burned out. You may miss hanging out, watching TV and sleeping longer. You may miss spending money on nice things, eating out, cable, and even taking trips. But you forego these things while you're pursuing financial freedom. You must make sacrifices with your time and money. Here's one adage I absolutely love, which I engraved in my thinking during the time I was going through the same process you're about to go through:

> Entrepreneurs do (in the beginning) what most people (employees) won't do, so they can be able to do (in five years) what most people (employees) cannot do (make that wake up whenever you feel like it money, give yourself a raise anytime you buy a property, earn passively so you can live passionately, receive mailbox money, pursue your passion).

Remember, these sacrifices are only temporary but the benefits last a lifetime. While it's perfectly fine to indulge in the finer things in life, only a small percentage of people will do the necessary things to become successful long-term. Only a small percentage of people are willing to apply the disciplines and make temporary sacrifices.

I made these sacrifices. I lived on a Ramen noodle diet. I avoided: hanging out, taking vacations, buying new clothes, buying a car while living in New Jersey, cable and other luxuries because I had a bigger goal in mind. If you're broke, you shouldn't spend your money on cable, Netflix or any other streaming device. That's a luxury you cannot afford, so cut it off! Use that spare time to apply the principles and disciplines outlined in this book. Continue to make temporary sacrifices until you reach financial freedom. Once you achieve financial freedom, you can PILE up.

As discussed in chapter one, PILE is an acronym, which means your passive income is greater than your living expenses. When I quit my job and moved to Atlanta, I had 30 rental units. With each property I purchased, I improved my standard of living. I bought a nine-unit property to afford my car note, gas, and insurance for my recently purchased

Mercedes Benz. I bought a six- unit property so I could take a vacation once a month. I bought an 11-unit property to solely pay off credit card debt with the rental income I received from that property. I bought a 13-unit property and another nine-unit property to increase my standard of living. I had to hire a property manager, two bookkeepers, as well as a housekeeper to clean my house since I dread doing domesticated activities. I'd rather buy properties so I can afford to hire people to do the "dirty" work. You can do the same! Focus on buying more real estate so you can improve your quality of life.

Again, give yourself a raise every time you close a deal. Every property I purchase with or without using my own money frees up my time because I outsource the mundane tasks. This allows me to pursue my passion—which is educating the masses and providing them with the tools to succeed financially. Today, I still don't watch cable television. I can afford it, but it's still a large waste of my time. You can pursue this lifestyle, as well. I'm glad that I applied those disciplines and made those sacrifices.

If you're not committed to applying the disciplines and principles to making these small temporary sacrifices, then put this book down and donate it to somebody who will. If you're dedicated, keep reading.

# SECOND ROADBLOCK:
# Running Out of Gas Money

In September of 2012, I saved enough money to purchase a quadplex. I was up to seven rental units in my portfolio; but I was nowhere near my financial freedom goal and this was my third year of real estate investing. I had just turned 29 years old, and I only had one more year left before quitting my job at 30 years old.

After closing on the quadplex, I attended my real estate networking group later that month. I discussed how I acquired the quadplex, the financing involved, obstacles I ran into, and how I overcame those obstacles. As a member, you had to share the details of your deal in front of the entire group so you could receive unbiased advice. It also served as a learning experience for everyone.

*Running Out of Gas Money*

After presenting the details of the deal to the group, Duane, my mentor, asked me, "How much additional passive income do you need per month in your portfolio to quit your day job?" I only needed an additional $2,000 a month in passive income to leave my day job and be comfortable. He looked at me in surprise and yelled, "Man, that's easy! The only thing you have to do is buy a ten-unit apartment building, assuming it is cash flowing $200 a month per unit."

> 10 units x $200 Cash Flow per unit =
> $2,000 per month in Cash Flow

I thought Duane was crazy. It took me three years to get seven rental units, and here he was telling me it was easy to get another ten units in one year. No sooner than I started doubting his advice, I instantly arrested my thoughts and remembered the Bible verse: *"If two or three agree as touching, anything they ask will be done unto them."* (Matthew 18:19 KJV) Inwardly, I agreed with Duane and said, "I am going to do it! I do not know how I am going to do it, but I will find out how."

I attended the same networking group every single month for three years. When I first subscribed to Duane's website, there were 600 members.

However, only six of us showed up consistently. I called us The Consistent Six. Out of the six, we all achieved our goals in various industries—some in real estate, some in franchises, some in restaurants and some in coffee shops. Out of the six, three of us formed our own accountability group. We met in person biweekly to discuss each other's short-term goals. If you are serious about quitting your job, stop hanging around employees all day long. Hang with entrepreneurs on a consistent basis. You become just like those you associate yourself with. If you hang with the wise, you will become wise. If you associate with fools, you will suffer harm *(He that walketh with wise men shall be wise: but a companion of fools shall be destroyed.* Proverbs 13:20*)*. Hang with real estate investors, and you will become one in due time.

Shortly after the meeting, I received a book in the mail from my mom as a birthday gift. I didn't pay much attention to it until Hurricane Sandy hit the New York/New Jersey area soon after. During the hurricane, all electricity and phone lines were out, and the city suspended public transportation for a week. As a result, I was stuck at home for a week. I took the book my mom sent me, lit a candle, and began reading. The book was *"Think and Grow Rich"* by Napoleon Hill. I read the book, although the language was difficult to understand at times.

After reading it, I did everything the author said to do—everything. I thought, "What do I have to lose? If the author said it worked for over 500 people, and they all became wealthy, then why not try it?"

A few months later, I took a trip to Atlanta to visit family and friends. Some of my long-term friends whom I knew since middle school urged me to play basketball at an outdoor court. While playing, someone stepped on my heel, and I fell to the ground. I thought I twisted my ankle. I blew it off and flew back to the New York/New Jersey area, still injured. When my ankle hadn't healed within a week, I went to see my doctor and discovered that I ruptured my Achilles tendon. I had to undergo surgery and could not walk for two months. Gratefully, I had enough sick time in which I could capitalize. But, that time also gave me more time to make myself wealthy—an extra 40 hours a week of spare time!

While sitting at home with my leg elevated, I conducted extensive research. Since I was immobile, I had to find and finance homes, and close all deals, remotely. I had to conduct my real estate investing business like an entrepreneur, not a self-employed person.

A self-employed person thinks they have to do everything. They work to find the deal, finance the deal and manage the deal until the end. A self-employed person brings all of these things to the table using his/her own means. However, this way takes forever to become financially free and independent.

An entrepreneur is the synergistic glue that brings all of the pieces together. An entrepreneur quarterbacks everything and does not have to perform every single duty out there on the field. An entrepreneur outsources. I had to be a real estate entrepreneur!

The two-month period of being immobilized did wonders for my real estate investing career. It truly was a blessing in disguise. I discovered what I needed to do to prevent running out of cash: finance deals 100% (The 100 Percent Financed Way). If I can finance the income-producing asset 100% and still make cash flow, there is no limit to how many deals I can close. I knew now what my new job description would be as a real estate entrepreneur: Get access to deals and get access to capital. Everything else gets outsourced.

Many of us believe that it takes money to make money. I think it takes creativity coupled with bravado to make money. *If the old adage holds true, guess what? It does not have to be your money! Having access to the capital is what matters. Banks are in business for lending money! As long as you improve your credit before you petition banks, the banks will see you as an attractive borrower and you can receive all the capital you need.*

While I continued to improve my personal credit, I discovered that I could use hard money and mortgages to purchase single-family homes, and use business credit, and seller financing for multi-unit properties. Hard money is considered a value play, while a multi-unit is a yield play. Value plays can be profitable, but there are greater risks because you usually deal with full rehabs. A full rehab is when a complete renovation needs to be done (everything from the basement to the roof).

Yield plays are less risky, but they give you cash flow on day one of closing. A yield play is an investment term that means you buy an asset that is already yielding profits day one of closing. A value play is when you buy a distressed asset that is not yielding much profit immediately since you need to do repairs, improve the occupancy, etc. to add value.

The hard money model works in the following scenario: buy the ugliest single-family house in the best neighborhood. Using hard money for single-family homes is great because a hard moneylender

(HML) may provide you with 100% financing. The HML will give you money to buy, fix up, and even close on the property if you can get these total costs below 65% - 75% ARV. ARV is an acronym for After Repair Value, which is what the house will be appraised at after the repairs are completed. As a conservative investor, I prefer to keep the cost below 70% ARV or lower.

Let's say you found a distressed house in a nice neighborhood. If neighborhoods rank from A, being the most desirable neighborhood to live in (new construction, nice restaurants, ideal location) to D, the less desirable (not safe to live in, low income, old buildings), let's say this house was in a B area.

After the house is fixed up, let's assume the value would be $100,000. Let's also assume this house is a Real Estate Owned (REO) or bank-owned home. You're able to purchase it at $25,000 from the bank using hard money, which is a cash offer. The house needs $35,000 in rehabilitation to beautify it, and the closing costs are $5,000.

> Total cost: $25,000 + $35,000 + $5,000 = $65,000

The total cost is 65% of the ARV, and most HMLs will give you 100% financing. A few may still require a down payment so that you can have "skin in the game." The good thing is that they do not verify the source of funds. You can get the down payment from a partner, private lender, savings, retirement account, or from a business credit card. Remember, you will have to pay holding costs. These costs hold the hard money loan. You will have to pay a hefty interest payment, as well as utilities, as long as you maintain the hard money loan. Your primary objective is to get into the hard money loan, and out of it, as soon as possible.

No HML is the same. HMLs have different requirements in different areas. Again, they are private lenders that lend in local markets and they can create their own lending criteria. If you want to invest in single-family homes the 100 Percent Financed Way and need a hard money loan, I suggest visiting www.100percentfinaced.com to see the resources we have for hard money loans; or you can reach out to 10 different HMLs. Look at their terms, and go with the one that you qualify for and has the best terms.

They are called HMLs for a reason. The terms are hard: 8% interest rate or higher, two points or higher, interest-only payments, prepayment penalties, application and upfront fees. Oftentimes, they'll want their principal back in a year's time. Even though the terms are hard, I still prefer it because you can get sweet cash flow in these deals once you refinance out of the hard money into a conventional mortgage. If you are using hard money, make sure you know all of the terms (interest rate, points, estimated closing costs, draw payments, prepayment penalties, upfront fees, down payment, how much of a hard money loan you qualify for, and minimum monthly payment). Make sure you get pre-qualified for an investment mortgage before you find a deal. Your goal is to use hard money to finance 100% of the cost, and then refinance it into a conventional investment mortgage. Obviously, you want to know the terms of the investment mortgage (previously listed) upfront to calculate your cash flow analysis.

I found a REO for $32,000 (purchase price). The house needed $50,000 worth of repairs. I ordered an appraisal, and the appraiser asked me what type of work I intended to do to the property. The appraiser is in a position to let you know whether value will be added to the property or not, based on the repair or improvement you plan to make.

Make sure the work you do to the property adds value to the (ARV). If adding a deck in the back costs $3,500, it will increase the house's value by $5,000 and that is a great value play. If adding a half bath downstairs costs $2,500, yet increases the property's value by $4,500, that is a great value play. If adding marble floors costs $10,000, and makes the value of your house higher than the competition (comparable sales), considering no other house has it, that may be a bad value play when selling a house.

The HML gave me the money to buy it and fix it up, but I had to come out of pocket $6000 to cover closing costs; however, no down payment was required since I was able to factor the purchase price and repair costs below 65% of the ARV. My application fee was $25. The interest rate was 15%, and there were two points. I had a six-month prepayment penalty and interest-only payments. The HML charged me two points instead of one since I was new and out of state. I was paying close to $1,000 a month in holding costs, and I used business credit to finance these holding costs.

After I fixed up the property, I placed a tenant in it who paid $1,550 a month for rent. I went to my mortgage lender and refinanced out of the HML via cash out refinance. I pulled out $27,000 cash. (This is a loan, not capital gains, by the way). Therefore, it's better than flipping because I don't have to pay a capital gains tax on the equity I pulled out; plus, I get to keep the property for cash flow.

The terms of my investment loan were amazing: I had a 5% interest rate, which was amortized over 20 years. My debt service payment dropped dramatically, and I cash flowed $600 a month off this one unit!

I put $6,000 of my own money into the deal and ended up pulling out $27,000 from the equity as a loan. I used a portion of that $27,000 to pay down business credit debt, and I used the rest for down payment money toward my next deal. If you want maximum cash flow per unit, use hard money for distressed single-family homes.

Errol, a former coaching student, found a hard money deal via networking with a team of listing agents. See the numbers below:

1. Purchase price: $100,000

2. ARV: $270,000

3. Down payment: $17,663

4. Appraisal: $390

5. Closing costs: $2,470

6. Other costs: $2,900

7. Monthly hard money payment: $541

8. Monthly investor loan payment: $135

Errol found an investor in a real estate investing group who wanted to get started in real estate, but did not have any experience. Errol informed the investor that he could provide him with hands-on experience if he invested with him. Errol was committed to managing the project, formulating a team and getting the approval for hard money. The partner would finance the total out-of-pocket costs not covered by the HML (down payment, appraisal, closing costs). Both Errol and the partner would split the monthly hard money payment and other holding costs (utilities). When it was time to do a cash out refinance, the investor will receive his total out-of-pocket costs back, plus $135 each month it took to get out of the deal. Then, Errol and his investor would split the remaining cash out refinance, as well as split the cash flow 50/50. Both Errol and the partner agreed, and went to an attorney to draft the agreement.

Everything is negotiable. Every deal is different. Every investment is different. Every market is different. Every financial instrument is different. Have the wisdom to determine how you can structure a deal so that everyone wins. Errol did an excellent job in structuring this deal. It provided him with a lot of work. He had to be onsite at least three times a week. He did, however, face some obstacles. Errol and his general contractor did not obtain a building permit, and the city inspector issued a stop work order until he got one. Make sure you get the necessary permits and work with qualified contractors who are insured and bonded.

As you can see, hard money can still be a good way of earning passive income, but it can take some time.

I prefer to only work with multi-unit deals since it requires less of my time in contrast to using hard money. You need to be onsite at least three days a week. It is a safer investment since you will be cash flowing day one of closing, and you can be a bit more creative. If you do not have multi-unit deals that you can afford in your market, you can either stick to the hard money model, or consider investing in multi-units out of state.

With multi-units, you can be a bit more creative with the financing. You can have the seller finance 10% of the down payment; you can use partnerships to qualify for commercial mortgages, as well as to help with the down payment. The underwriters for commercial mortgages are less stringent than residential underwriters. Plus, you can leverage economies of scale. Why buy 10 single-family homes in 10 separate transactions, when you can potentially buy 10 units under one roof or in one portfolio? You may obtain less cash flow per unit in contrast to using hard money for single-family homes, but you can close on these deals a lot quicker. If you're buying a property using a hard money loan and doing a full rehab, you will have holding costs. If you buy multifamily properties fully occupied with tenants, you will be cash flowing day one of closing. Plus, the repairs are cosmetic, so there is less risk.

Between the two 100% financed strategies, I prefer the multi-units. Large numbers sound attractive to investors when raising capital; however, what really matters is your cash flow and return, not the number of units.

After discovering and implementing these strategies, not only did I accomplish my goal of obtaining 10 rental units, but I obtained 13 additional units. By February of 2014, I had 30 rental units in my portfolio. It was time to submit that resignation letter, the same one I drafted after being reprimanded by my supervisor for my out-of-the-box thinking.

If it's taking time to repair your credit and to acquire funds for total out-of-pocket expenses, you can still complete real estate investing deals with partners. However, you must bring something to the table for these partners to work with you. In all real estate deals, each party has to bring at least one of three things to the table:

1. **Time:** Hours, knowledge, resources, connections with professionals in the industry (real estate agents, mortgage lenders, appraisers, real estate attorneys)

2. **Appearance (looking good on paper):** Decent FICO score, low DTI, no losses on tax returns, global income

3. **Out-of-Pocket Money:** Liquid funds to cover down payments, closing costs, reserves, and soft costs (attorney fees, appraisals, property inspections)

If you don't look good on paper, or if you don't have the out-of-pocket money, you'll have to bring your time to the table. While you are fixing your credit and networking to find partners, make sure you learn all you can about real estate investing and network with professionals in the industry. In a short amount of time, you will look good on paper, have the out-of-pocket money, and be able to bring your time to the table. You will be unstoppable.

Ahmad, a former coaching student of mine who lives in Boston, MA found a great quadplex in the Boston area via the Multiple Listing Service (MLS).

He looked good on paper; he used a FHA mortgage to cover 97.5% of the loan amount, and he financed the down payment, soft costs, and closing costs with business credit. After discussing the cash flow analysis with him via our scheduled one-on-one coaching call, he was cash flowing $500 a month after all expenses, debt service, and reserves were allocated. He lived in one unit and rented out the others. If you are using business credit for a residential mortgage (1-4 units), make sure you have the business credit funds in your bank account for approximately two months (two bank statements) to meet most mortgage lenders' seasoning requirements. If the lenders ask where the funds came from, you can say they are business funds.

Next, we'll cover what makes a deal a deal in multifamily investment and the business model you should implement as a multi-unit real estate investor. If you're interested in obtaining multi-units in the same market I invest in, then our Multi-unit Acquisition Program (MAP) may be of interest to you. Our MAP is a full service program in which we offer cashflowing rentals to investors who bring the appearance and out-of-pocket money, but just don't have the time. Check out 100percentfinanced.com for more information. Also, check out

100percentfinanced.com for additional real estate coaching programs we offer.

##  KEY PRINCIPLES

- **Find the silver lining.** There is always a silver lining. Search for it.

- **Seek and you will find.** *Proverbs 25:2:* It is for God to conceal a matter, but for kings to discover it. If you want to be great, search and find the resources you need to accomplish your goals.

- **Be positive.** Don't think about why it can't be done; think about how it can be done.

- **Apply the instructions you receive in books.** If the author gave you a plan of action based on his research and experiences, why not take advantage and implement it?

- **Think creatively.** Think outside the box.

- **Are you an entrepreneur?** Being an entrepreneur is not the same as being self-employed.

- **Play it big.** Do not be afraid to play a bigger game and go to a new level. Challenge yourself. If you are accustomed to closing on single-family homes, acquire a duplex. If you are used to duplexes, buy a quadplex. If you are used to quadplexes, buy a ten-unit property.

- **Keep an open mind.** If someone more experienced than you says you can do it, move forward in it.

- **Network.** Attend at least two networking events a month, one for real estate investing and another for personal development. If you find active real estate investors in these groups, take them out for coffee and pick their brains. Don't let me, Juan Pablo, be your only mentor. You need a local mentor, as well. Again, use your spare time wisely to make yourself wealthy.

- **You become like those whom you most associate yourself with.** If you are not associating with entrepreneurs on a consistent basis, how can you expect to become a successful one?

# THE FIRST M:
# The Model

Now that you know how I acquired enough rental properties to quit my day job in a short time, I will teach you how to do the same. First, you have to know *"The 3 Ms."* The first **M** is **The Model**.

Not every property is a deal. Since I am an online entrepreneur, in addition to being a full-time real estate investor, I receive numerous questions like:

*What are your thoughts on investing in storage facilities?*

*Is investing in office space a great investment?*

*What about mobile homes and foreclosures?*

There are many vehicles you can take on the road to financial freedom. However, each vehicle must satisfy the following criteria to be considered a deal:

1. Cash flow of at least $100 per unit
2. 100% financed
3. Ability to increase value

##  CASH FLOW

I mentioned cash flow earlier in a sense that was synonymous with passive income. Cash flow is a form of passive income because it is rental income you receive on a consistent basis (monthly) with little to no work required. You must calculate the cash flow on every deal that comes across your table.

> Cash Flow = Gross Revenue - Vacancy Rate - Operating Expenses - Reserves - Debt Service

For example, let's assume you receive a listing from a real estate agent for a duplex. See the listing below (in monthly totals).

– $1,000 in rent ($500 rent for each unit)
– 5% vacancy rate ($1,000 x .05 = $50)
– $45 coined laundry

- $85 property taxes
- $45 hazard insurance
- $25 water
- $15 caretaker (seasonal lawn maintenance)
- $10 pest control
- 10% maintenance reserve ($1,000 x .10 = $100)
- $400 mortgage (principal and interest payment)
- $75 investor loan (money from an investor to finance the down payment. Interest only payments)

> Cash Flow = ($1,000 + $45 laundry) - ($50 + $85 + $45 + $25 + $15 + $10 + $100 + $400 + $75) = $240

**Cash Flow = $240 a Month in Passive Income**

I always recommend your cash flow (profit in your pocket) be at least $100 per unit. If you come across a similar deal, and it cash flows less than $100 per unit, you may still want to consider the deal if you are using little to none of your own money. Also, consider closing the deal if there are no other more profitable options available. It's all a plus. If the cash flow breaks even, or has a negative cash flow, do not continue with the deal. If your realtor tries to sell you on pro forma (what the numbers could be), or on the appreciation rate when the property has a negative cash flow, don't go through with it. There are plenty of cash flowing deals from which to choose. Why settle for one that does not cash flow?

## 100% FINANCED

In the above example, let's say the duplex costs $85,000. If you bought this with a residential investment mortgage, you would have to bring a 20% down payment of $85,000, which equals $17,000. Since we also have to factor in soft costs (appraisals, property inspections, attorney's fees and two months operating expenses for reserves, which equates to $2,500), and closing costs (closing attorney's fees including title work, realtor fees and lender fees, which equates to $3,000), we now need $22,500 ($17,000 + $2,500 + $3,000) to close this deal. To purchase this property 100% financed, an investor will lend you $22,500 at 4% interest-only payments, with a balloon payment in five years ($22,500 x .04)/12 months = $75 per month. Because the interest rate is low, he also wants to get paid two points. A point is 1% of the amount of money borrowed. So, if you owe this private lender two points, you owe him an additional 2% on top of the money you already owe him ($22,500 x .02 = $450) at the end of the five years when the balloon payment (remaining balance) is due.

Don't get me wrong; there is nothing wrong with using your own cash in a deal. I did in the beginning. But, I kept running out of cash since I was dependent on my savings to finance the total out-of-pocket costs for a deal. If you feel more comfortable having skin in the game, make sure you obtain a minimum 10% cash-on-cash return on your money invested. The cash-on-cash return (yearly cash flow/total out-of-pocket cash) is a great tool to use to compare the profitability of other assets. It lets you know how much bang you get for your buck. If I was entertaining two different deals—one with a 14% rate of return and another with a 16% rate of return, I would select the one with the highest cash-on-cash return, which is 16%. Our MAP offers a minimum return of 15%.

If you use your own cash in this scenario, your yearly cash flow would be (subtract the investor loan payment):

✓ Cash flow = ($1,000 + $45 laundry) - ($50 + $85 + $45 + $25 + $15 + $10 + $100 + $400) = $315

✓ Yearly cash flow = $315 x 12 months = $3,780

- ✓ Total out-of-pocket = $22,500
- ✓ Cash-on-Cash Return = $3,780/$22,500 = 16.80%

A cash-on-cash return of 16.80% exceeds the 15% benchmark, which is pretty good. Nevertheless, if none of your cash is in the deal, what would be your cash-on-cash return?

- ✓ Yearly cash flow = $240 x 12 Months = $2,880
- ✓ Total out-of-pocket = $0
- ✓ Cash-On-Cash Return = $2,880/$0 = Infinite Return on Investment

In this scenario, you are generating a cash flow of $240 per month, with none of your money in the deal. This is the true meaning of the term 100% financed. You are making money without using your money. It throws the old adage, "It takes money to make money" out the window! However, you'll still have to pay the investor back $22,950 ($22,500 + $450 = $22,950)! This leads us to our third criteria.

## INCREASE VALUE

Leverage is the name of the game. You can leverage one asset to help you get into another by increasing the value of the asset enough to tap into the equity.

## Here are three ways to increase value:

1. Buy the asset with built-in equity.

2. Force the appreciation.

3. Acquire natural market appreciation.

It's important to increase the value so you can either pull out the equity to pay off an investor ($22,950), or use the capital as down payment money for your next deal. In this example, we will use a cash-out refinance to pay off our investor.

1. **Built-in equity.** In the above example, we purchased the asset for $85,000. As a real estate investor, you should always buy a property less than what the asset is worth. Always aim to buy it with 20% built-in equity, but settle for no less than 10%. Let's say you buy it with 15% built-in equity ($85,000/(1 - .15), which equals $100,000). The appraisal comes back at $100,000, but you have the duplex under contract for $85,000. To do a cash-out refinance with most mortgage lenders (at the time of this writing), you will need 20% built-in equity. Here is the formula for a cash-out refinance:

> (Appraised Value x .80) -
> Mortgage Loan Amount – Closing Costs =
> Cash-Out Refinance Amount

*The Model*

Our mortgage loan amount is $68,000 ($85,000 x .80). We can't do a cash-out refinance after closing because lenders have seasoning requirements (normally six months to a year). Let's say we waited a year, and paid down the mortgage to $65,000. We can do a cash-out refinance!

> $100,000 x .80 = $80,000
>
> $80,000 - $65,000 = $15,000 - $1,950 Closing Costs = $13,050

We would use this $13,050 cash-out refinance to pay down the investor loan. We would owe the investor $9,900 ($22,950 - $13,050). How else can we pay off the $9,900 before it matures in five years?

2. **Force the appreciation.** When we acquired this asset, and performed our financial due diligence by verifying the income and expenses, we discovered that Section 8 pays $600 per unit for a two-bedroom, two-bath apartment. We are currently earning $500 per unit. When the current tenants' leases expire, we should submit rent increases, or politely ask them to vacate with proper notice to find a Section 8 tenant. Let's say we found two new Section 8 tenants within a year's time. We have now increased our revenue by $200 a month! What is our cash flow now?

- ✓ $1,200 in rent ($600 rent for each unit)
- ✓ 5% vacancy rate ($1,200 x .05 = $60)
- ✓ $45 coined laundry
- ✓ $85 property taxes
- ✓ $45 hazard insurance
- ✓ $25 water
- ✓ $15 caretaker (seasonal lawn maintenance)
- ✓ $10 pest control
- ✓ 10% maintenance reserve ($1,200 x .10 = $120)
- ✓ $400 mortgage (principal and interest payment)
- ✓ $75 investor loan (money from investor to finance down payment. Interest-only payments)

> Cash Flow = ($1.200 + $45) - ($60 + $85 + $45 + $25 + $15 + $10 + $120 + $400 + $75) = $410

Not only did we increase your monthly cash flow by an additional $170 per month, but you also increased the value since the profitability of this asset has now increased as a result of a rent increase. Because the value increased, we can now pull even more cash out of equity. Let's assume the appraised value is no longer $100,000, but now it's

$110,000 as a result of the rent increase. In the built-in equity example, we used a $100,000 appraised value. What if we used the $110,000 value, keeping everything else the same? What would be our cash-out in this situation?

> (Appraised Value x .80) - Mortgage Amount = Cash-out Refinance Amount minus closing costs

> $110,000 x .80 = $88,000. $88,000 - $65,000 = $23,000. $23,000 - $2,250
> Closing costs = $20,750

Closing costs will increase since the loan amount increased. We would use this $20,750 cash-out refinance to pay down the investor loan. We would now owe the investor $22,950 - $20,750 = $2,200. There are other ways we can pay off the investor loan.

We can also increase value by reducing expenses. If we added water conservation kits, and reduced our operating expenses and debt service, we would also make this asset more profitable.

3. **Natural market appreciation.** You should always buy a property in a natural appreciating market. The value is just increasing based upon what's going on in the market. Let's say the

housing market in this area had an appreciation rate of 2.5%. Assuming the value was $110,000 based on forcing the appreciation, the value would now be $112,750 ($110,000 x 1.025). How much equity would we be able to pull out via cash-out refinance?

> Cash-Out Refinance: $112,750 x .80 = $90,200. $90,200 - $65,000 = $25,200. $25,200 - $2,550
>
> Closing costs = $22,650

We would use this $22,650 cash-out refinance to pay down the investor loan. We would now owe the investor $300 ($22,950 - $22,650). I am sure you can scrape up $300 from your sock drawer to pay off the investor.

It's important to have more than one exit strategy to pay off the investor loan. The market may tank and there won't be any appreciation. What if you do not qualify for a refinance later down the road?

One key principle is, if you don't need it, don't eat it. In year one, you cash flowed $2,880 ($240 x 12 months). You increased the rent in year two. In years 2-4, you generated $14,760 in cash flow ($410 x 12 months) x three years. Total cash flow year one, plus total cash flow for years 2-4 equals $17,640.

*The Model*

Again, **if you don't need it, don't eat it**. Do not spend your cash flow. Continue to reinvest it to pay off the investor loan. Save it for your next deal, or use it to improve your personal credit. If you use this $17,640 to pay down your investor loan, you will only need to scrape up an additional $5,310. Hopefully, the market does not crash in five years, and you will be able to refinance. However, it's always good to have more than one exit strategy in place.

If you bought the property with built-in equity, forced the appreciation, bought in a natural appreciating market, and saved 100% of your cash flow in four years, you could potentially pay off the investor loan in full and have $17,340 ($17,640 - $300) left over for down payment money for your next deal. During this time, you could be cultivating more investors, as well as reaching out to your current investor for your next deal. You could potentially close a bigger deal since you now have access to more capital.

If we do a cash-out refinance, and pay off the investor loan, the cash flow will differ since we have a different mortgage amount. Mortgage amount would no longer be $65,000, but $90,200. Hence, the monthly mortgage payment would increase. We no longer have to pay the investor loan amount of

$75 since the investor is now paid in full. Always update your cash flow analysis every time your income, expenses, or debt service changes. Lastly, you are increasing rent on a yearly basis (place this in your leases), so you should be in good shape.

Since you are just starting out in real estate investing, I recommend you pursue yield plays instead of value plays. In yield plays, you buy 100% occupied at closing. These properties already have tenants occupying the spaces. As soon as you close, you know how much money you are going to make. Investing in yield plays is a safer investment strategy because, many times, the properties don't require major repairs. Value plays, on the other hand, are distressed assets that need major repairs (over $5,000 in repairs per unit). If you only have single-family homes in your market, value plays make more sense. With this investment strategy, it may take several weeks or months to prepare the property for rent. Hard money is usually used in this model. Starting out, you may not know much about full rehabs, or even have a qualified general contractor that you can trust. It's easy to get burned in this model. Plus, if you are inexperienced, you may underestimate the repairs, over-repair, overestimate the value, and underestimate the rehab time. These estimates can equate to more money out of your pocket, which will reduce your bottom line. If you want to do value plays, wait until you have done a few yield plays and have found a reliable contracting team.

In the above scenario, you qualified for an investment mortgage and you were able to convince an investor to lend you the remaining funds needed to finance the deal via a promissory note. Being that you provided the investor a promissory note, he is, in essence, a lender and does not have any ownership (or equity) in the deal. What if an investor wants equity instead of just interest rate and points? What if you cannot qualify for a mortgage? If you cannot qualify for a mortgage, but have a network of people who would love to invest with you, you can do a partnership. If you cannot qualify for a mortgage, and you do not have a network of people who can qualify, you can do a master lease option.

I recommend doing a partnership with five or more units. Reach out to your local real estate attorney on the specifics of setting up one. With partnerships, you are the general partner: the entrepreneur, the quarterback, and the head coach. With partnerships, you can be a part of a multifamily deal without having to qualify for a loan, as long as you limit your ownership to 19% or less. Financing changes and each mortgage lender have different criteria, so it is your responsibility to verify this information with your mortgage broker. Not only can you obtain 19% of the cash flow for putting the deal together as the partner, but you can also receive an acquisition fee of 1-3% of the purchase price. For example, if you purchase a six-unit apartment for $180,000, a cash flow of $900 per month, and an acquisition fee of 3%, you would own 19% of the property. You will also receive 19% of the cash flow, which equals $171 ($900 x .19). You will receive an acquisition fee of $5,400 ($180,000 x .03).

You have to make sure your partners qualify for the mortgage and that they have the funds to cover the total out-of-pocket costs. Again, you can bring your time to the table and still make money. Investors would be willing to partner with you as long as you are perceived as credible. They want to be sure you are trustworthy. There are many investors and partners who do not have the time or desire to learn real estate investing, but they perceive the value in it. Therefore, they will be willing to partner with someone who can bring their time to the table.

A master lease option is an agreement in which you control the asset, but do not own it. You are under a lease with the seller, with an option to buy it later. A seller who will be willing to make this type of arrangement is usually highly motivated. This person is in a "need to sell" position, not a "want to sell" or "it will be nice to sell, but I am not in a rush" position. If the seller owns multifamily real estate, he or she may be a bit savvier than a seller who owns a single-family home. So, you have to become savvier yourself to convince the seller to do a master lease option.

Typically, a master lease option is broken down into two documents: a master lease and an option to purchase. With the master lease, you control the asset. You collect all rent, pay all bills, make all repairs, and oversee the property management. You are in full control. However, you do not own it. The seller still benefits from the tax write-offs, but you can potentially benefit from the cash flow.

With a master lease option, typically you will have to provide an option similar to a down payment. You want to cash flow your option back in half the time. For example, if you have noticed that the cash flow for the year is $12,000, and you have set a lease option for four years, your option amount should be no more than $24,000. The great thing about master lease options is that no banks are involved, so everything is negotiable.

In 2015, I had two deals under contract. I came across another deal, a 13-unit apartment building with a new listing agent. The listing agent informed me that the seller hired a property manager to manage and repair the property. The property manager would also be responsible for collecting all cash payments, and must use the cash payments to manage the property (evictions, notices) as well as to repair the property. The owner had Section 8 tenants in which Section 8 paid half of the rent, and the tenants were responsible for paying the other half with cash. The owner used the Section 8 money to pay the bills (mortgage payments, insurance, taxes, and utilities). The property manager was responsible for collecting the cash payments directly from the tenants. Whatever cash payments were left over went into the property manager's pockets. The property manager quickly realized that the fewer repairs he made, the more money he kept in his pockets.

As a result, the property manager did not perform any repairs. If he did, he used cheap material. Therefore, tenants became disgruntled and only complained to the property manager. Of course, he did not inform the owner. Tenants moved out and occupancy decreased. With this knowledge, I told the listing agent that a Master Lease Option (MLO) was the best solution since my mortgage lender would not provide me a mortgage as a result of the state in which the property was in.

I informed the listing agent that since an MLO is not a sale, I would still pay him $2,000 for his time if we closed. I needed him to convince the seller that this was the best option. The listing agent agreed. I told the listing agent to have this conversation with the seller, and if he was interested in learning more, we could schedule a three-way conversation. Always speak with the seller to establish rapport.

We had the three-way conversation, and I advised the seller of the particulars. As with every negotiation, I immediately stated the worst-case scenarios with the other party, and how it would be more of a benefit to them than it was to me. My goal was to increase occupancy and complete repairs, so why would I make the property pretty and not buy it at the end of the option period? Worst-case scenario, the seller would receive the property back, with all repairs completed and higher occupancy rates. Because I was in control, I was responsible for paying all bills and for conducting repairs. If he found out the bills were not being paid, and the repairs were not being made, a clause within the MLO states that they could take me to court and kept my option.

I answered all of the seller's concerns, and we proceeded with the MLO. I reached out to one of my real estate attorneys to draft the MLO document. We set the option amount at $12,000 since our lease option period was two years and the property cash flowed about $12,000 for the year. I also mentioned to the seller that I would pay him $400 a month for allowing me to do this option, but half of this payment would be credited to my down payment if I decided to exercise my option. We also set the terms of the option when I decided to exercise my option to buy it. We set a purchase price, and he agreed to do seller financing.

I ordered a property inspection. I used this as a bargaining piece to reduce my option amount. I told the seller the repairs were more than I anticipated, so I wanted to provide a $6,000 option instead of a $12,000 option. I also wanted to waive the first year's payments ($400), to which he agreed. I was still credited on paper for a $12,000 option, and for $200 a month the first year to go towards the down payment, if I decided to exercise my option.

We closed; I paid the listing agent $2,000 and fired the property manager. I immediately made repairs and filled vacancies. However, we ran into an issue with the deal. The 13-unit was split into a nine-unit and a four-unit. The city wanted the seller to demolish the four-unit. The seller agreed, which made our contract null and void. Unfortunately, I couldn't exercise my option to buy it since we couldn't agree on a fair price for the remaining nine-unit. Not every deal is a good deal, but every deal is a learning experience. At least I was able to cash flow my option back and get out the deal without issues.

##  KEY PRINCIPLES

- **Fall in love with the numbers, not the property.** If the numbers don't work, move on to the next deal.

- **Think logically.** The decisions you make in real estate investing should always be logical, never emotional.

- **If you don't need it, don't eat it.** Keep investing in real estate while working your day job. All profits you receive from real estate investing should be reinvested to pay down debt or increase your real estate holdings.

- **Evaluate all consequences up front.** As you can see in the above examples, extensive analysis was completed before we even looked at the property or placed it under contract. Know all the numbers before you sign on the dotted line.

- **Have an abundance mentality.** Plenty of deals fit your investment model; you just have to find them.

- **Network all the time.** Tell everyone you meet that you are a successful real estate investor. If people are interested in investing in real estate, invite them to join your free "Biweekly Real Estate Educational Call" to educate them on investing in real estate. After a period of two months, present a call-to-action to get a deal done.

- **Sweeten the deal.** If working with investors or partners, find out what they want in the deal and make it sweet for them. After all, they are enabling you to obtain an income-producing asset, 100% financed.

- **Create multiple exit strategies.** As soon as you come in the front door, think about the back door. Think about the windows, too. Have multiple exit strategies in place to exit out of expensive financing before you purchase the property.

# THE SECOND M:
# The Market

You may want to consider multifamily investing. But first, determine which market you will invest in to obtain these properties. Are there multifamily properties in your area? If so, can you afford them?

Throughout the remainder of this book, I'll be using multi-family and multi-unit interchangeably. You can find the definition of each word in the glossary at the end of the book.

## Criteria for investing in multifamily properties:

1. C neighborhood transitioning to a B neighborhood

2. Cap rate of 10% or higher

3. Max $35,000 per door price

4. Blue collar area

5. Low crime

Neighborhoods are ranked on a level of A, B, C and D. Neighborhood A is the area with Whole Foods, fancy yogurt spots, and people jogging at night. Neighborhood D areas have old buildings, less desirable tenants, higher crime rates, and areas a person may feel unsafe while walking at night. Neighborhood A areas are safer investments and may produce a lower return for the cash invested. Neighborhood D areas may offer the highest cash-on-cash return, but may be a headache to manage. Neighborhood A areas tend to appreciate higher, but cost more money to get into. Neighborhood D areas appreciate at a much slower pace, yet cost less to get into. I prefer C areas because it's low income (Section 8 is great) and the crime rate is low. Plus, I can get more "bang for my buck" (higher cash-on-cash return), and it's affordable.

Cap rates let you know the profitability of a market. The higher the cap rate, the higher the profitability for a market.

*Here are some formulas you need to know:*

| NOI = Value x Cap Rate |
|---|

Net Operating Income = All revenue from property minus All reasonable operating expenses and reserves (does not include debt service)

> Cap Rate = NOI/Value

The cap rates let you know how profitable and/or risky a market is. See the cap rates below.

> Value = NOI/Cap Rate

Location matters, but if you know the NOI from the property and the cap rate in the area, you can estimate what the value of the property will be with this equation. That way, you can know upfront if you are buying the property with built-in equity.

## Below are the normal cap rates for an area.

A. 4–6%

B. 7–9%

C. 10–12%

D. 12%+

These figures can change. You can obtain a C property at a 9% cap rate, or a C property at a 13% cap rate depending on the NOI and the price. The above numbers are just benchmarks. I like to buy multifamily properties (five or more units) for $25,000-$35,000 per unit. I would pay more if I could afford to and if I received a cash-on-cash return that is 10% or higher. If the market you live in does not have multifamily properties you can afford, or the market doesn't have small multifamily properties, invest outside your market or buy several single family properties as a package in one single transaction (multi-unit portfolio).

I had to do the same. I lived in the New York City area and the price point was too high. I bought a duplex for $355,000. While attending a networking event, Duane encouraged Steve, a fellow member of the group who had just closed on a six-unit apartment building, to discuss the numbers of his deal. After Steve finished, I immediately approached him.

I took him out to lunch and asked the following questions:

1. How did you get started?
2. What are your interests?
3. Why did you choose this market?
4. What type of properties do you normally purchase, and are there multifamily properties in this market?
5. What is the average price per unit, cap rate and class of neighborhoods?

6. What contacts do you have that you don't mind sharing?

Steve shared his investment model and market, and he also shared a few contacts with me. If you are undecided about which market to invest in, attend a networking event, socialize with everyone, and see what attendees are buying. If you find someone who has a bigger portfolio than you, invite that person out for drinks, coffee or dinner. Make sure you foot the bill. Establish rapport. Ask about his or her successes. Ask about their market, model and contacts. Once you "interview" several movers and shakers, you can decide which market is most profitable for you.

I cannot stress the importance of networking enough. You can learn real estate investing by watching a YouTube video or reading a book, but there's nothing like connecting with real people. People will share their experiences and contacts that pertain to your market. More than likely, you won't find this information in a book sitting at home in your PJs.

If you don't encounter anyone who invests out of state, consider joining other networking events in or outside your market. If you find an investor in your market who is more experienced than you, ask him/her to mentor you. You can find networking events by searching your city name alongside "REIA" (Real Estate Investor Association or Real Estate Investor Alliance), or searching "Real Estate Groups" on Google or Meetup.com. Another way to research a market is to look at Marcus and Millichap and other real estate research companies.

Don't be afraid to invest outside your market. Again, I lived near the New York City market and invested in a market six hours away. As long as you run your real estate investing business with the mindset of an entrepreneur, you will soar. Focus on doing two things well: access the deals and the capital, and outsource everything else. I will show you how you can access capital in the next chapter.

##  KEY PRINCIPLES

- **Know your market.** If your local market has high price points or no multifamily inventory, explore other markets.

- **It's all about the numbers.** The property does not have to look pretty, but the numbers must look pretty. As long as the deal meets the three criteria, and the property is up to code, go for it.

- **Network, network and network!** Don't feel inferior when you reach out to those who have a bigger portfolio than you. You will catch up to them soon. Take them out and treat them in return for picking their brains and their Rolodex.

- **Select the right market.** An emerging market is a market that's transitioning to a better neighborhood. Low income, but low crime is the sweet spot. Make sure your C areas are in emerging markets.

- **Who said you had to use your own money?** Always remind yourself that you are a real estate entrepreneur. You can own properties anywhere and fund deals without using your own money.

*The Market*

# THE THIRD M:
# The Money

"Show me the money!" is a famous line from the movie, *Jerry McGuire*. Real estate professionals will perceive you as credible if you show them the money (i.e., a prequalification letter from your mortgage company and proof of funds). After you have learned your multifamily investing model and market, focus on providing proof that you have the "capital" to deal with finders (real estate agents and wholesalers).

Most listing agents do not want to spend their gas or time showing property after property, only to find out you cannot qualify for a mortgage. Get qualified! Reach out to a mortgage broker (not a banker) in the market in which you plan to invest in. Provide him/her with your financials (tax returns, W2s, 1099s, PFS, etc.) and a copy of your recent credit report (no older than 30 days). Most mortgage brokers want to run a credit report using their credit monitoring system, but you can avoid a hard inquiry by presenting them with a recent copy of your credit report, using your own credit monitoring service. Assure the broker that if you qualify based upon your financials, you will grant him/her permission to run your credit using his/her system. It does not make sense to have the broker run your credit, only to tell you that you do not qualify.

Persistence is key in this game. Real estate investing is a people-based game and a numbers game. You may have to reach out to several brokers. If you have to reach out to ten, reach out to ten. Find the one who will look at your finances and tell you whether you qualify for a mortgage or not. Obtain a pre-qualification letter. In the commercial world, some mortgage lenders do not do pre- qualification letters. In that case, ask the lender if he or she will vouch for you if you provide the listing agent the lender's contact information.

If you do not qualify for a mortgage, it's not the end of the world. Ask the broker what you need to do, specifically, to qualify. If you need to reduce your debt-to-income ratio, determine how much you need to reduce it by in order to qualify. If you have to increase your FICO score, determine what FICO score you need to qualify. If you need to partner with someone who looks good on paper, consider bringing in a partner. Don't let anyone deny you without specific reasons.

If I advise a layperson to get pre-qualified for a mortgage, and the layperson does not provide the specifics, I get disappointed. If this person tells me he/she doesn't qualify because their DTI is 65%, and it needs to be 45%, we implement a plan to obtain that 45%. If the layperson simply says, "My DTI is too high," I'll respond, "Well, what is your DTI currently and what do we need to get it to?" When the layperson says, "Uh, I do not know," the layperson is wasting time. Always obtain the specifics.

If you qualify, great job! Request a prequalification letter and know the terms (how much of the purchase price you can buy, the minimum payment of the mortgage, interest rate, points, estimated closing costs, etc.). Unfortunately, not all mortgage brokers provide a pre-qualification letter. No worries, ask the mortgage broker to send you an email detailing the mortgage amount you can potentially get qualified for.

You also need to ascertain where you are going to get the total out-of-pocket money you need. Wherever you get it from, you must be able to show proof (of funds) to the listing agent. That way, a listing agent knows you have money and will find a deal that fits your budget. Concerning total out-of-pocket costs, you can show proof using yours or your partner's bank statements, retirement accounts, or business income.

With every multi-unit deal, make sure you structure the deal to have the majority of the financing come from the following sources:

1. Mortgage: 80% of the purchase price. Most mortgage lenders require the property to be at least 80% occupied. However, you can place contingency in your purchase and sale agreement to have the property 100% occupied at closing.

2. Seller Financing: 10% of the purchase price. In regards to the terms of the Seller Financing, I request 5% interest rate and a 10-year amortized balloon payment in five years. You can negotiate different terms with the seller, but make sure the property still cash flows and that you have more than one exit strategy to get out of the seller financing when the note is due.

So far, you're at a total financing amount of 90% of the purchase price. But, you still need access to additional funds (total out-of-pocket costs) to close the deal.

By the way, if you own 19% or less equity, mortgage lenders don't need to see your financials if you're going forward with a multi-family deal. One last thing about mortgages, many investors have a hard time obtaining a commercial mortgage due to a lack of real estate experience; this matters to most lenders. You can get around this by working with commercial mortgage lenders. In our MAP, we have our preferred portfolio lenders (along with vetted vendors) who will provide you with a commercial mortgage regardless of experience.

## Total Out-of-Pocket Costs Needed:

1. 10% down payment

2. 7% soft costs (appraisals, property inspections, attorney's fees, traveling expenses, acquisition fees if syndicating the deal, and reserves)

3. 3% closing costs (lender fees, title work, and real estate agent fees)

4. Total financing: 20% of purchase price. As you can see, you want more than enough money to cover the down payment, soft costs, and closing costs. Where are you going to get the rest of the money to cover the total out-of-pocket costs?

## Sources to Finance Total Out-of-Pocket Costs:

1. Savings. Again, make sure your cash-on-cash return is at least 10%

2. Retirement accounts

3. Private partner, owns equity

4. Private lender, only provides a loan with no equity

5. Business credit. Apply for a free consultation at http://100percentfinanced.com

6. Rent Proration. If the property is 100% occupied at closing, and you close on the third day of the month, the seller would get prorated three days of rent, and you will get prorated the other 27 days of rent (assuming there are 31 days in the month) at closing. That way, you make money at closing. This is real estate investing at its finest, folks. If you are supposed to bring $55,000 to the closing table, and had a rent proration of $4,500 credit, you now have to bring $51,500 to the closing table.

7. Security deposit credits. If the seller has $5,000 in security deposits, you will receive them at closing as a credit. If you are supposed to bring

$51,500 to the closing table, and had a $5,000 credit for security deposits, you now have to bring $46,500 to the closing table.

8. Repair allowances. If you find that there are much-needed repairs on the property worth $7,500, negotiate a repair allowance. Have your contractors (not the seller) fix the repairs. At closing, if you are supposed to bring $46,500 to the closing table, and have a $7,500 repair allowance, you now need to bring $39,000 to the closing table.

One way to finance total out-of-pocket costs not listed above is through personal credit cards or personal line-of-credit. You should never use personal debt to finance deals. I learned this the hard way. I made the fatal mistake of using personal debt to finance the repairs on the second deal I bought in Pittsburgh in December 2010. I used a refinance from a car I owned free and clear to assist with purchasing the house (this is okay). Then, I obtained a personal line of credit from my credit union and used personal credit cards to fix up the house (this is not okay).

After completion of the rehab, I placed a tenant in the home, and went to my mortgage broker to do a refinance. After going through the refinance process, and spending money to order an appraisal, the house appraised at $70,000. I invested roughly $35,000 in this property. Unfortunately, the refinance was halted for having a high debt-to-income ratio. My debt-to-credit ratio and my debt-to-income ratio was above their qualifying criteria since I charged my personal line-of-credit and personal credit cards (about $25,000 in total) to finance the repairs. Not only was I still figuring property management out and saving for down payments, but I also had to pay down my personal line of credit with the credit union. I also had to pay my personal credit cards for my debt-to-income ratio to reach most mortgage lenders' standards. Again, I do not recommend using personal revolving debt (lines of credit or credit cards) to finance out-of-pocket costs. However, installment debt (pulling cash out of an existing house or car) is recommended. Business credit is a much better source for funds.

Business credit does not show up on your personal credit report as an account, but it does show up as an inquiry. The good thing is you can dispute the inquiry via credit repair.

Considering the business credit account does not show up on your personal credit report, you can max them out for your deals. Additionally, you can apply for another round of business credit every three to six months. So, you can always have another source of funds to cover your out-of-pocket expenses.

If you are using business credit to cover your out-of-pocket expenses, it's important for you to convert it into cash. Here are a few ways you can convert business credit into cash:

1. **Convenience checks.** You need at least one major credit card with at least a $5,000 maximum limit. If your credit cards with major banks are not sending you convenience checks, request them. Once you deposit the convenience checks into your business checking account in the amount of $5,000, you now have $5,000 charged to your personal major credit card. Next, call the customer service center on your business credit card and request a balance transfer from your personal credit card to the business credit card.

2. **Balance transfer checks.** You need at least one major credit card with at least a $5,000 maximum limit. If your credit cards with major banks aren't sending you balance transfer checks, request them. Once you deposit the balance transfer checks into your business checking account amounting to $5,000, you now have

$5,000 charged to your personal major credit card. Next, call the customer service center on your business credit card and request a balance transfer from your personal credit card to the business credit card. As you can see, the process for convenience checks and balance transfer checks is the same.

3. **Cash advances.** You need at least one major credit card with at least a $5,000 maximum limit that allows cash advances. Most major credit cards have a limit of how much you can take out as a cash advance. So, make sure you call and confirm the maximum cash advance you can take in one day. When you go to the ATM and make a cash advance, deposit the cash into your business checking account. You now have the cash advance amount charged to your personal major credit card. Next, call the customer service center on your business credit card and request a balance transfer from your personal credit card to the business credit card.

We, at 100PF, have helped real estate investors and entrepreneurs obtain well over a million dollars worth of business credit through our program. Many secured the funding they needed within 30 days of applying. We have had a 26-year-old client without a ten-year credit history receive over $50,000 in funding. A coaching student received over $98,000 in financing. We have even helped an aspiring entrepreneur with a 680 credit score, and 40% DTC ratio obtain $8,000. Eight thousand may seem small, but at least he was able to get his foot in the door. Now, we can teach him how to request credit line increases, apply for multiple rounds of business funding, foreign file in other states, and create new entities—all to obtain more funding.

Starting out, I had a 680 credit score, an eight-year credit history, a DTC of over 40%, late pays and collections on my credit report. I was awarded $6,000 and quickly talked my way up to $10,000. Many people are unaware that you can immediately call your business credit cards and request increases, as soon as you receive the business credit cards in hand. Now, I have well over $200,000 available in business credit that I can use for obtaining properties, as an operating account to pay for marketing expenses, and/or to use as an emergency fund. We all start somewhere. Even if you are not close to qualifying for business credit, still apply to receive the free consultation. Apply now at www.100percentfinanced.com.

As soon as you have acquired the necessary funds, move forward to find deals. If it's taking you months to get the money together due to challenged credit, no net worth, no partners, no mortgage pre-qualification letter, no proof of funds and no down payment money, do not fret. No one ever said something worth having comes easy. Real estate investing is simple, but it's not easy. It takes a burning desire and tenacity to stay committed. Although this book serves as the blueprint, you still must do the work. If you are feeling discouraged or burned out, stay at your day job. I had to reach out to many mortgage brokers. I received several mortgage denial letters in the mail, but I refused to be discouraged.

I have lost money in this game. I've had contractors rip me off, as well. If you have a burning desire for this business, you will shake those things off and keep going. Simply having the desire to be a full-time real estate investor means you are capable of doing it. It took me two years of credit repair to finally qualify for a mortgage. Just stick with it.

## KEY PRINCIPLES

- **Prove credibility.** When adding new members to your team, it's important that you prove credibility.

- **Follow up.** As with all sales jobs, the key is following up. Often, you will have to follow up several times for mortgage brokers and listing agents to work with you. If five do not return your call after several attempts, reach out to five or ten more until someone answers the phone and is willing to work with you.

- **Partners equal access.** You do not have to have the money, but you do need to have access to it. That's the purpose of partners.

- **Take action.** Gather the specific reasons as to why you didn't qualify, and take action to correct those issues that are holding you back from getting qualified.

- **Use various resources.** You can use a mixture of various sources for the total out-of-pocket costs. Just make sure the property still cash flows, and you have multiple exit strategies to get out of short-term or expensive financing.

- **Keep your personal credit healthy.** Make sure you don't have derogatory items on your credit report. Have at least one credit card with a $5,000 limit with a major bank, and keep your debt-to-credit ratio below 30%.

- **Use the banks' money for real estate investing**. What do you think the banks are in business for? They are in business to lend you money.

# Deal Finders

Now that you have proof of funds and a pre-qualification letter, it's time to present these items to a deal finder. Deal finders are listing agents and wholesalers who find deals. Wholesalers are real estate investors who find deals and will assign their contract to you for a nominal fee. They market for a deal, place it under contract, and sell their contract to you. I like working with wholesalers since they have the mindset of an investor. Plus, their assignment fee is negotiable. You can find wholesalers at real estate networking events and by responding to those "We Buy Ugly Houses" billboards. Wholesalers are perfect for finding distressed single-family homes for the hard money model. You can also use listing agents to find distressed single-family homes using homepath.com, auction.com, or by networking at your local real estate investing group. When wholesalers assign their contract for a fee, they use this money to invest in real estate once they are qualified for a mortgage. If you do not have the credit or money for all of your out-of-pocket costs, consider wholesaling. We will discuss wholesaling in another chapter, then you can become a deal finder and make money without much cash or credit.

Conventional wisdom tells you that you should work with a buyer's agent since you buy real estate as an investor. But, you should primarily work with listing/seller's agents. There are several reasons why:

1. Listing agents know the condition of the property.

2. Listing agents know the motivation of the seller.

3. Listing agents represent the seller. However, if they represent you as well, there is no other barrier between you and the seller.

4. Listing agents represent more than the seller. If they represent you, the listing agent acts as a dual agent. As a dual agent or transactional broker, the listing agent gets both sides of the commission. Therefore, he/she doesn't mind bargaining back and forth with the seller to reduce the purchase price or offer seller financing. The listing agent would rather receive 6% commission of a $100,000 purchase price than 3% of a $150,000

purchase price. This can work out for you since you will be able to have a covert agent on your side to help you get the purchase price and terms you want.

5. Listing agents will perceive you as a repeat customer. Therefore, the listing agent will reach out to you first for future deals rather than posting the deal on loopnet.com or any other multiple listing service. This connection is called a pocket listing. Pocket listings are great since it eliminates competition. I primarily work with listing agents in contrast to wholesalers, and I only close on deals that are pocket listings.

If your investment strategy is multifamily investing, I recommend you go on loopnet.com, search for multifamily properties in the zip codes in which you intend to invest, and write down the names and phone numbers of every agent you find. You can also find deal finders at real estate networking events. You can also search "commercial real estate agents" in your city and state using your favorite search engine.

Gather a list of 25 listing agents/wholesalers, then cold-call all of them. Call them first instead of emailing them. Start the conversation by introducing yourself. Then, tell them you want their email address to send them your proof of funds, pre-qualification letter, and other financial documents (PFS, credit report, bank statements, and retirement accounts). If you do not have a pre-qualification, send them the name, email and phone number of the mortgage lender you are working with.

Also, tell your deal finders the kinds of deals you are looking for (model). Ask them if they have any of these types of deals in their inventory. Find ways to establish rapport. Make sure you keep adequate notes because you always need to follow up. Don't be discouraged if you never hear back from a deal finder after your initial call. Everyone in the industry isn't as ambitious or as professional as you. You will have to follow up with them. Normally, a deal finder will add you to their email list and automatically send you deals. For the purpose of establishing rapport and following up, call the deal finder after every email blast. Thank the deal finder for sending you the deal and, if it is a good deal, ask about the numbers and put it under contract. If it is not a good deal, thank him or her and remind him or her of the kind of deal you prefer. Again, establish rapport. You are more likely to build rapport via phone than over email. Meet the deal finder in person, if possible. Your goal when adding someone new to your real estate investing team is to prove that you are credible and likable so they will work with you.

Out of every 25 deal-finders, maybe eight of them will send you profitable deals. You may do the majority of your deals with four or five deal finders. Remember, real estate investing is a game of numbers and people. You may have to review a few hundred deals to find the deals that will help you achieve financial freedom. Plus, people like to work with their friends. I cannot stress enough the importance of being likable and establishing rapport. Don't be difficult to work with. Be a person of your word; be professional and be likable. If deal finders find you credible enough to close deals, and you are a pleasure to work with, it's a done deal.

When you start receiving deals, this is known as deal flow. If you have eight deal finders who send you deals consistently, it could be time-consuming to analyze every single listing. Therefore, apply the 1% rule. The gross monthly rent should equal 1% of the purchase price. If you are buying a duplex for $85,000, the monthly rent should equate to $850 collectively. In our scenario in a previous chapter, the gross monthly rent before we increased it was $1,000 collectively, so this passed the 1% rule.

If the 1% rule does not work on a deal, look at another. If your top eight deal finders send you ten deals each, that's 80 deals. Apply the 1% rule to all of them. Let's assume that two out of ten deals pass the 1% rule. Eighty deals x .20 equals 16 deals. Place all 16 deals in the cash flow deal analyzer (subscribe to www.100percentfinanced.com to obtain a free copy) to make sure the deals cash flow. If they cash flow over $100/unit, reach out to the deal finder immediately to inquire more and potentially submit an offer or letter of intent (this is also available to all who subscribe to 100PF). Write offers on the deals that have a cash-on-cash return of 10% or higher. Of all the deals that have a cash-on-cash return of 10% or higher, three of your offers may get accepted and you will close on one. Again, real estate investing is a numbers game. Typically, we offer a 15% return in our MAP.

Keep in mind, if you cold-called 25 deal finders, and none of them reach out to you, reach out to another 25 and consider investing in a different market. Lastly, analyze what you may be doing wrong. Perhaps others don't perceive you as credible. Perhaps you didn't research your market, and the deal finder can sense that. Maybe you have not built rapport or you're not polite. Perhaps you didn't prove credibility on the initial call by providing them with copies of your Personal Financial Statement (PFS), proof of funds and pre-qualification letter. Don't give up until you cultivate your team. Be tenacious and stick to the script.

 **KEY PRINCIPLES**

- **Persistence is key.** Be politely persistent until you achieve the desired results.

- **Real estate investing is a numbers-based, people-based game.** You may have to cold-call several people. When you find someone who is willing to work with you, sell them on the fact that you are credible and likable.

- **Keep building your team until you find the right people.** The hardest part of getting started is the constant follow-up. Once you have built your team, it's all gravy from there.

- **Scared money makes no money.** If you are scared to cold-call, take a personal development or business course.

- **As an entrepreneur, you need to perfect two essential skills: the ability to sell and the ability to raise capital.** Use these in every business endeavor you encounter.

- **Duplication is better than innovation.** If your mentor created a system that works, why not duplicate it? Do not try to innovate without guidance. Sure, you may eventually gain success, but you may experience a ton of bumps and bruises along the way. A mentor is your shortcut to success. Follow his/her instructions, even if it doesn't make sense in your mind. Don't be afraid to challenge your mentor.

# Deal Analysis
## *Closing a Deal*

You are making great progress! By now, you have deal flow coming in, and you are applying the 1% rule. For those properties that meet or exceed the 1% rule, you have to analyze the cash flow, just like we did in Chapter 4, *Running Out of Gas: Feeling Burned Out.*

## Remember the following three criteria:

1. Cash flow

2. A minimum cash-on-cash return of 10%

3. Increase value

If you make an offer on a multi-unit property, submit a Letter of Intent (LOI). You can find a sample letter of intent at www.100percentfinanced.com.

## *Items to include on the LOI:*

1. Purchase price should have 5-15% built-in equity. If you estimate the value of the property to be $100,000, negotiate a purchase price of $85,000 to $90,000.

2. Earnest money should be $2,000 max.

3. Seller financing should be 5-8% interest, amortized over ten years with a five-year balloon.

4. Due diligence is 45 days.

You may have to go back and forth with the seller over the purchase price and terms outlined in the LOI. Please understand that you may not get everything you want in negotiating. For example, if the seller wants a 9% interest rate, and you only have 9% built-in equity, but the property still satisfies the three criteria, consider closing the deal.

As soon as your offer gets accepted, place the following contingencies in your contract:

1. **Title contingency.** If the title work is cloudy (seller has judgments or issues with ownership), you can back out of the deal without consequences.

2. **Appraisal contingency.** If the appraised value is less than the purchase price, and the seller refuses to reduce the purchase price to meet the

appraised value, you can back out of the deal and receive your earnest money deposit back.

3. **Financing contingency.** If you do not qualify for a mortgage, you can back out of the deal without consequences.

4. **Documents.** The seller must provide the following documents within five business days of executing the contract:

   a. Seller tax returns for the past two years, reflecting operating expenses for the property

   b. All leases

   c. Rent roll

   d. Trailing 12 of all utility bills the owner is responsible for paying; the Trailing Twelve Months (TTM) refers to the last 12-month period for a selected expense. So, if I'm buying a property in March of 2017, I want to see the past utility bills from March 2016 to February 2017.

   e. Profit & Loss statements

   If the seller does not provide all documents within five business days, do not submit your earnest money deposit to your real estate agent or closing attorney. I normally send my earnest money deposit to my closing attorney instead of my real estate agent.

5. **100% occupied.** Make sure properties are 100% occupied at closing (no vacancies).

Make sure you are quarterbacking this whole deal. Have your partners provide documents to the real estate attorney, as well as to your mortgage lender, to form an entity. As soon as you receive the documents from the seller, submit the earnest money deposit to your closing attorney and start the financial due diligence immediately. Compare the numbers found on the listing against the seller's documents, and also compare these against the third-party companies. For example, if the listing states that the taxes are $3,500 for the year, look at the seller's tax returns to confirm. Also, call the local tax office (third party company) to verify the information.

## *Perform the financial due diligence for all of the numbers:*

1. Rents & leases

2. Taxes

3. Insurance (obtain an insurance quote from your insurance broker)

4. Utilities

5. Property management (if you choose not to self-manage the property)

6. Other (lawn care, snow removal, pest control, alarm system, legal fees, admin fees, phone fees, etc.)

If there are major discrepancies (the listing overestimated the income or underestimated the expenses by over $500 for the year), ask the agent to ask the seller to provide an explanation. If the explanation is inadequate, you may have to negotiate purchase price during the financial due diligence period. Simply explain that you performed due diligence and the numbers are not adding up. You wrote your offer based on the numbers found on the listing, which will provide a certain return on investment. Because your return on your investment may be lower because of overstated income and understated expenses (without a valid explanation), you need to reduce the purchase price so you can still maintain the same rate of return for your partners.

You're doing due diligence on all of the income and expenses, and you're completing it within 15 days of executing the contract. After completion of the financial due diligence, it's time to start the physical due diligence. As you noticed, I did not advise you to look at the property, write an offer, and ask for the numbers. I advised you to run the numbers (financial due diligence) first. This way, you don't waste time or money visiting the property (traveling expenses) or ordering a property inspection.

After the financial due diligence checks out, and you have 30 days left in the due diligence period (15 for financial due diligence and 30 for physical due diligence), to visit the property and order a property inspection. Make sure you see every unit. If the tenants changed the locks without notifying the proper authorities, clearly state that you have to see the unit or you will have to back out of the deal. You never know if the owner or current property manager is trying to hide something. I learned this the hard way. We thoroughly perform due diligence for our MAP clients.

I was under contract to buy a six-unit apartment building. The owner walked me through four of the six units. He assumed the tenants changed the locks. I ordered a property inspection a few days later, and the inspector mentioned that the two units I did not get to see had sagging floors, which meant major foundational issues. If I could have looked at those units, I may have noticed the sagging floors and pulled out of the deal before spending money on a property inspection.

The property inspector should detail the report, outlining all issues with the property, from the basement to the roof. Once you have the property inspected, address all of the main problems (roof, mechanical, plumbing, electrical, foundation, environmental). Have your contractor, HVAC contractor and/or plumber provide you with quotes for these repairs. Present the property inspection report, along with the contractor's bid, to the listing agent so that he/she can pass it along to the seller. Tell them you want credit (repair allowance) at closing for all major repairs. Get the seller to sign a document agreeing to the repair allowance. Send this to your mortgage lender and closing attorney. Always have your contractors perform the repairs, not the seller's contractors. If the seller and his/her contractors do the repairs, they may do a cheap or shoddy job. You should have your team of qualified contractors perform the repairs.

While you are completing the physical due diligence, check in with the title attorney and mortgage lender to see if there is anything else they need from you or your partners. Keep your partners abreast of each stage of the process. Make sure they have their total out-of-pocket liquid funds in their bank accounts approximately a month before closing. Ask them to send you proof. Again, your job as a real estate entrepreneur is to make sure everything is moving along smoothly. If something slips through the cracks, it's not the other party's fault; it's yours.

Your lender should provide you with a mortgage commitment letter verifying that you and your partners are qualified for financing. Afterward, your lender will notify you when to pay for the appraisal. It may take two to three weeks for the appraisal report to come back. If the appraisal comes back with a value below the purchase price, the seller would have to lower the purchase price to meet the appraised value, or you will have to back out of the deal. If the appraisal meets or exceeds the purchase price, you can close.

Before closing, you should receive the HUD (settlement statement), which outlines all closing costs and how much the buyer (you and your partners) should bring to the table. According to Wikipedia, the HUD-1 Settlement Statement was a standard form in use in the United States of America, which was used to itemize services and fees charged to the borrower by the lender or broker when applying for a loan for the purpose of purchasing or refinancing real estate. Security deposits and rent proration should be accurately outlined. I always aim to close the first week of the month, so I can get the full month's rent credit at closing. If you have not noticed, repair allowances, security deposits, and rent proration reduces the total amount of out-of-pocket funds you have to bring to the closing table.

Finally, notify the tenants of the new property management company if you decide not to keep the current management company. If it is a small apartment building (ten or fewer units), manage it yourself. If it is greater than ten units, screen a reputable property management company to maintain it for you. The property management letter you provide to the current tenants should outline how to pay rent, the contact information of the managers, how to submit repair requests, and special nuances about the new management company. Remember, I owned 30 rental units while still working a full-time job, and I managed the units myself. Once I quit my full-time job, I decided to outsource property management. Manage your own units to keep operating expenses low.

You can close in person or remotely. After you close, make sure you obtain all keys and make sure they work. Host monthly calls to update your partners of the cash flow and other pertinent information for the property. Be very transparent and pay your partners on a timely basis.

You may be in a position where you currently do not qualify for financing, you don't have any funds to cover out-of-pocket expenses for closing, and you may not have any partners who are willing to invest with you. It's okay; we all start somewhere. While you are increasing your knowledge, networking, and perfecting your credit via credit repair, use your time to wholesale real estate to generate funds. Proceed to the next chapter to learn how you can make money off real estate via wholesaling.

##  KEY PRINCIPLES

- **Everything is negotiable.**
- **Don't be afraid to place those contingencies in the deal, or back out if the numbers do not work.** Don't be greedy or back out because you have cold feet. Deal finders will lose interest in you.

- **When I say the property has to be 100% occupied at closing, I mean that.** Do not compromise. If there is a vacant unit, wait to close until after the seller fills that vacancy.

- **Be the quarterback.** The ball is in your court, so make sure you touch base with everyone in the deal to make sure they are doing their part.

- **Trust, but verify.** During the due diligence phase, you transform from the investor to an investigator. Investigate everything.

*Congrats on closing your first deal! If you would like additional help acquiring a multi-unit deal, go to http://100percentfinanced.com to learn more.*

# Wholesaling Real Estate Without Cash or Credit

You may not qualify for the buy and hold strategy just yet. You may not have the credit score, the debt-to-credit ratio or the out-of-pocket closing. However, if you have time, you can make money off real estate via wholesaling. Wholesaling does not require a credit check or down payment. However, it does require your time and your ability to network.

If you have the time, the credit and/or partners, you may not have to wholesale real estate. If you're in a position to buy it, the buy and hold strategy will get you closer to financial freedom. Therefore, you can skip this chapter and proceed to the following chapter. However, if you're looking to get access to additional capital to fund your deals, you may want to entertain wholesaling a few deals to build your cash reserves. Wholesale four deals and use the proceeds to fund your next buy and hold deal. Again, do not eat the profits you receive from your wholesaling endeavors. The profits are seed money.

You should have multiple ways to get access to cash. If your time permits, wholesale to build cash reserves to fund your buy and hold strategy. If your credit permits, use business credit to build cash reserves in 30 days or less to fund your buy and hold strategy. If your network permits, ask partners and private lenders to fund your buy and hold strategy. Partners and private lenders may be cheaper than business credit and it doesn't take as much time as wholesaling; however, most partners and private lenders want to work with someone with a proven track record. If you're just getting started, why would they want to partner with you on your buy and hold strategy if you have bad credit and no proven track record? If you're in this position, do a few wholesale deals and share your experiences with your partners and private lenders. For example, let them know you've done ten real estate transactions which profited you $50,000, and share the details. As you can see, wholesaling real estate has its benefits. Now, it's time for you to learn how to wholesale real estate.

A wholesaler is an investor who signs a contract to purchase a property from a seller, then enters into an agreement with a third party to resell the same property at a higher price for a profit. The wholesaler assigns all rights of the original purchase contract to the new buyer, and the new buyer pays an "assignment fee" to the wholesaler to gain all rights to purchase the property at the original purchase price. The original purchase contract usually has an "inspection period," which allows the wholesaler to back out of the contract. They will not close on it if they do not find a buyer to assign their contract. Many wholesalers have no intention of actually purchasing the property. They only use wholesaling as a tool to locate properties for other investors or rehabilitators. Wholesalers who can identify good investment opportunities for other investors can make a living by finding these properties and assigning the rights to the buyers. The name of the game is marketing and networking. The only costs involved in these transactions are marketing costs. Therefore, a wholesaler has minimal risk since he or she is not required to put a down payment.

Some people think wholesaling is fraudulent misrepresentation since the wholesaler does not intend to close on the property. However, wholesaling is perfectly legal in the United States, and every real estate contract allows the buyer an inspection period. Many industries outside of real estate participate in wholesaling. When done successfully, the seller is unaware that the wholesaler did not purchase the property. But do you think the seller cares whose name was used to close on the property? The seller is simply happy that the house sold and could care less who bought it.

In this chapter, we will show you how to locate single-family homes that need repair before reselling it for a quick profit. You will learn how to find motivated sellers and buyers, and everything in between.

## *Wholesaling is ideal for you if you:*

✓ Have bad credit, no documented income, and losses on tax returns

✓ Do not have enough money to cover out-of-pocket costs (down payment, soft costs, closing costs)

✓ Do not have a network of people who are willing to bring their credit or money to the table to partner with you on a deal

✓ Have the time to market and network

✓ Have at least $1,000 for marketing purposes

Wholesaling is a means to an end, but not the end. While you are wholesaling, save cash, improve your credit, and network with partners so you can eventually get into the buy and hold game.

Just to give you an idea of how quickly you can start making money, take a look below:

✓ The wholesale process takes 30-90 days to close on your first deal.

✓ A wholesaler works approximately five to ten hours per week.

✓ Wholesalers earn $2,000-$20,000 per deal. You can expect to make $5,000 per deal on average.

These reasons make wholesaling the highest paid (dollar per hour) job in real estate. If you have a day job, wholesaling can take some time. There are two valuable resources in this world: time and money. If you don't have the money to buy cash flowing rental properties, you better have the time to wholesale these deals to those who can. Wholesaling can be done on a part-time basis, as long as you have a sound marketing strategy. Wholesaling is a job; it is not considered passive income. It is quick income. If you do not wholesale, you do not eat. If your goal is to quit your 9-to-5 soon, use the proceeds of each wholesale deal toward the down payment on rental properties or to improve your credit score (pay down debt or hire a credit repair company) so you can qualify for mortgages and business credit. Use your quick income to finance your passive income. With passive income from rental properties, rent checks still arrive in your mailbox every month, even if you don't wholesale a single property.

Most wholesalers start from scratch, without any money, bad credit and no prior knowledge of real estate investing. That's why it's important for you to network and work with other wholesalers. You may find a motivated seller, and another wholesaler may find a rehabilitator who wants the deal! Starting out, all you need is a desire to learn, mixed with a determination to make it happen. I am here to give you a realistic roadmap to get your first few deals.

## MINDSET

Mindset always trumps skill set. Your mind is the real key to breaking through and reaching your true potential as a real estate wholesaler. Most people give up on their dreams and personal goals prematurely because they cannot see past their current financial situation. Some people let others crush their dreams. Others cannot stay dedicated long enough. The reality is most successful people fail at some point when pursuing their endeavors. Most successful people go through many hardships and failures in their businesses and personal lives on their path to success. They don't let that stop them.

*The solution to their success is their ability to do two things:*

✓ Learn from their mistakes.

✓ Keep trying until they become successful.

Do you have what it takes to push through the pain of uncertainty, and the time it takes to get over your learning curve? Life will have ups and downs, and it may not be easy at times. Do your best to remain humble, coachable, and dedicated. You are on your way to closing deals and putting extra cash in your pockets. Let's get into the meat of the matter and show you how to locate these quick profit deals.

 **MOTIVATED SELLERS**

There are a few effective strategies for finding motivated sellers. First, let's define a motivated seller. A motivated seller is a property owner who is willing to sell their property for a very low price.

Oftentimes, they need to sell quickly because of the following reasons:

✓ Divorce or separation

✓ Bankruptcy or foreclosure

✓ Death in the family and they can no longer afford to live there or do not want to live there

✓ Job change/relocation and can no longer afford two house payments

✓ Change in employment status (laid off, downsized, or fired)

✓ Inheriting an unwanted property and do not want to be real estate investors

✓ The owner is a tired landlord who wants to get out of the real estate investing business

A wholesaler can market to these individuals and help alleviate them of the pain of owning unwanted property. This is where you come in to help solve some of their problems and make a quick profit.

# DRIVING FOR DOLLARS AND USING DIRECT MAIL TO FIND VACANT PROPERTIES

The first way to find motivated sellers is to start "driving for dollars." Driving for dollars is an excellent way to find pockets of real estate that are unlisted. You may find a sweet deal around the corner from where you live that is not listed with a realtor yet. This means less competition for you because the average real estate investor invests mostly online.

Find at least five to ten vacant properties. Take a pen and notepad with you. Do not drive in "war zones," but in working class neighborhoods. Keep an eye out for "For Rent" signs, overflowing mail, tall grass in the front yard, boarded windows, disconnected gas meters, fire damaged houses, and "For Sale by Owner" signs. Drive through areas you are considering investing in, and take different routes when driving home from work to scope out vacant properties. A good day to drive for dollars is on trash day. A vacant house will not have trash out consistently. Find as many vacant properties as you can, then look up the owner on the county's tax assessor's website. The website will let you know who owns it (person, investment company, or bank).

The mailing address and subject property address may not match at times. The houses owned by homeowners who live out of state are the best properties to wholesale. Look for a separate mailing address on the tax assessor's or county clerk of recorder's website so you can send a letter or postcard to express an interest in buying the property. If there is no separate mailing address, send a letter to the vacant property because that mailbox may have a forwarding address. How often should you send direct mail to a property you want to wholesale? It is entirely up to you and your marketing budget. One wholesaler spent $600 per month on marketing in a two-month period and closed on two wholesale deals for $9,500. You don't have to spend this much.

Connecting with all leads at least once a month is good. Make sure you are persistent. As soon as you find out who owns the vacant home, take a step further by looking up the property owner's phone number. You can also search for the phone number on anywho.com, whitepages.com, or 411.com. If an investment company owns the vacant property, send a letter to the mailing address.

As you drive for dollars, give the mailman your business card and tell him to call you if he finds a vacant house. Let him know you will pay him a referral fee as soon as the house is sold. That way, you are expanding your reach to have others find deals for you.

## USING THE COUNTY'S TAX ASSESSOR WEBSITE TO FIND MOTIVATED SELLERS

Go to the county tax assessor website and pick a target area to research. Click each property to see if the property owner's address is different from the subject property listed to find prospects. Property owners with a different mailing address than the subject property tend to be more motivated to sell (motivated sellers).

If the vacant subject property is 12345 Main St., Atlanta, GA, and the owner's address is 12345 Main St., Atlanta, GA, this may not be a prospect. But if the subject property is 12345 Main St., Atlanta, GA, and the property owner's address is 1110 Sellers Way, Orlando, FL, you may have a prospect. When you have a prospect or good lead, mail a letter to the property owner, expressing interest in purchasing the property. A sample letter for motivated sellers can be found in the appendix.

Looking through tax records can be time consuming. But, there are tons of list sites that you can use to get out-of-state access to owners who happen to be great leads. One website is www.listsource.com. For a one-time fee or a monthly rate, you can pull lists of out-of-state owners and properties that have a certain amount of equity. Send a letter/postcard to the owner.

With direct mail, you don't have to mail out each postcard or letter yourself. There are companies online that will do the legwork for you, such as www.click2mail.com. Click2mail.com helps save time. Simply upload the out-of-state owner list you compiled from listsource.com to an excel spreadsheet, and submit it to www.click2mail.com. That service will print the letter, place it in a stamped envelope, and mail it out for you. The old way of mailing letters still has its benefits. The letter can be typed, but if you address the envelope with blue ink and make it look personalized, you may receive a higher response from potential sellers. Also, signing your name in blue ink on the typed letter can increase your response rate. You can pay an employee $1 for every envelope that is drafted, signed, placed in an envelope, and mailed. The $1 includes labor and materials.

Using www.rocketprintandmail.com is another great resource for a direct mail campaign. They are a one-stop-shop for absentee owner lists. Plus, they also mail the letters for you! Of course, since they are a one-stop shop, they may be a tad more expensive than using listsource.com and click2mail.com.

##  USING THE INTERNET TO ATTRACT MOTIVATED SELLERS AND BUYERS

Before you attract motivated sellers and buyers online, set up accounts that are critical to your wholesale business. These accounts will be used for advertising and facilitating communications between you, the buyer, and the sellers. The great thing about most of these accounts is that they are free and easy to set up.

First, set up a Gmail account. You will run marketing campaigns for both buyers and sellers. To receive communications from your prospects, you will need to establish new emails and phone numbers. You will need *at least* two new real estate-related Gmail accounts that are easy to remember:

1. Create a seller Gmail account.
2. Create a buyer Gmail account.

An example would be 123jerseyhomebuyers.com for your seller email account. Now that you have a Gmail account, set up a Google Voice account that links to the email address. Google Voice offers you a free phone number (VOIP) for your email lines. Go to www.googlevoice.com. The site shows you how to set it up, step-by-step. Create a voice line for your buyer email account as well. Use the email address you created for the corresponding phone lines. Each phone line you create can be forwarded to your cell phone or your office phone. Once you set up your lines, go to the Settings tab in your Google Voice account and change your settings to suit your needs. You may want to set up the following:

✓ Call screening OFF (when people call it sounds like a regular phone line)

✓ Caller ID incoming

✓ Click: Display My Google Voice Number (Shows your Google Voice number when someone calls you. With this setting, you will know the call is about business)

- ✓ Caller ID Outgoing
- ✓ Click: Display My Google Number (Shows your Google number when you make outgoing calls. People will see your Google Voice number, not your personal phone number)
- ✓ Do Not Disturb
- ✓ For 'Missed Calls' Click: Place Missed Calls in the Inbox (Sends the missed call to your email so you can call them back, even if they do not leave a message)
- ✓ Click: Send Missed Calls to My Email: youremail@gmail.com.
- ✓ For 'Call Options', Click: Enable Recording (4), Switch (★) and Conferencing Options on Inbound Calls Global Spam Filtering (This will allow you to record important calls if you are out and about)
- ✓ Click: Send Calls and Text Messages from Numbers Identified as Spam by Google Directly to the Spam Folder (This will block unwanted SPAM, telemarketers and texts)

You also have to set up your classified websites so you can generate leads. It is important to let people know that you buy and sell houses online. If your phone is not ringing, you're not making money.

Craigslist is a great account to open. Create your Craigslist accounts at accounts.craigslist.org/.

A. **For your sellers:** Link to the seller phone line and the email you created above

B. **For your buyers:** Link to the buyer phone line and email you created above

Set up a Postlets account at http://www.postlets.com/signup.php. This site will post properties that are available throughout the internet on many websites.

Once you have this account set up, start attracting buyers and sellers to your phone line. You can view our Buyers and Sellers Sample Ads located in the appendix. These ads need to be posted daily, so they will always be on the first page of each classified website. Make sure you update the ad every three days. You can update it by changing the title. The more creative your headline, the more chances that you will receive a response from someone looking to sell. The "I Buy Houses" headline is okay, but it is very generic. Over 90% of wholesalers use this headline. Why would your potential seller choose you over the other 90%? If you were a potential seller and saw the headline, "Tired Landlord and Need Cash Now?" you may be inclined to click the ad. Try to use the seller's motivation (divorce, foreclosure, bankruptcy) in the headline.

## USING BANDIT SIGNS TO ATTRACT MOTIVATED SELLERS

Sometimes, you see signs on street corners and freeway entrances planted into the ground, attached to utility poles and fences, and sometimes stapled to trees. These are bandit signs. They serve as a very effective marketing tool. Bandit signs can put quick profits into your pockets. Plus, they may be more cost effective than having a direct mail marketing campaign. In fact, they may be the most effective of all marketing strategies. However, the downside to posting bandit signs is that in most municipalities, they are considered illegal and a nuisance (hence the name). Code Enforcement, the city department that attaches fines to homeowners and businesses for violations associated with city ordinances and laws, can be pretty innovative in setting up meetings with you to hand you a ticket. Keep this in mind if you plan to implement this strategy.

You can pre-order bandit signs or make them yourself. If you are starting with a minimal budget, it will be more cost-efficient for you to make your own.

We usually purchase our supplies at Home Depot, but you can go to your local hardware store and ask if they have corrugated plastic sheets. Large corrugated plastic sheets work best. If you go to Home Depot, ask if they have 48 x 96 inch white corrugated plastic cardboard in the shower accessories department. If they do not have sheets that size, ask to see the biggest sheets available. Do not go to the mailbox aisle or the "For Rent" sign area. You will be severely overcharged for the same materials.

These are the tools you will need if you plan on placing these into the ground. Slip the wire poles into the bottom of your bandit sign, and position your sign the way you want it to face. Step on the bottom ring to place it into the earth. These signs are easy to plant and easy to remove. Depending on what is more prevalent in your area, wooden utility poles, metal utility poles or open land, the way you post them will be up to you. The best place to post them is in high-traffic areas, like busy intersections and expressway exits. Placing signs next to high-traffic business entrances, such as grocery stores, gas stations, and shopping centers is also an excellent way to get your phone ringing. Again check with your local government before you post signs.

If you are in an area with lots of wooden poles, purchase a hammer stapler. This tool staples signs to poles and wooden surfaces fast. If you are in an area with lots of metal poles, use zip ties. You can attach your signs to metal poles and gates with these. If you poke two holes in the face of the sign with a screwdriver, run the zip ties through the holes. You can attach the signs to metal poles. These signs take time, but they last a lot longer because they are more sturdy. These signs last a lot longer than ground and stapled signs. If Code Enforcement orders you to take them down, you may be taking them down by yourself, or risk paying a fine.

Remember, bandit signs are illegal in most cities. Most Code Enforcement officers only work during the week, so a lot of wholesalers place them out on a Friday night and pick them back up the following Sunday. This will help you avoid calls and expensive tickets. Keep a list of where you place the signs in case you are called to remove them. Also, track your most effective traffic areas.

# 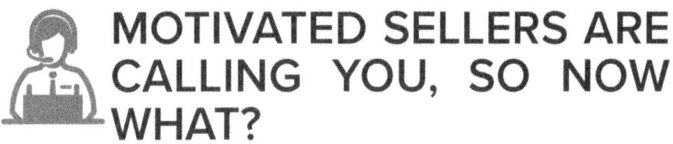 MOTIVATED SELLERS ARE CALLING YOU, SO NOW WHAT?

If your phone is ringing, that's a good thing. Now, you need to qualify your leads to see which ones are worth pursuing. You will have to do some research, possibly meet with the motivated sellers, and look at the property before you can get the motivated seller to sign the contract.

There are nine steps you need to take to close a wholesale deal with the motivated seller:

1. Have a conversation with the motivated seller, and use the script to screen the qualified leads.

2. Research the property to find out who owns it, and find out what's the ARV.

3. Set up an appointment to view the property and to meet with the motivated seller.

4. Visit the property to build rapport with the motivated seller, and come up with a repair estimate.

5. Go home and do your due diligence.

6. Calculate the Maximum Allowable Offer (MAO), and present it to the motivated seller.

7. Get the property under contract.
8. Send the contract to the title company.
9. Assign contract to a buyer (discussed in detail in the next chapter).

---

1. **Have a conversation with the motivated sellers.** Ask them to tell you about the property using the 100 Percent Financed Motivated Sellers Script. This is your opportunity to get valuable information about the property before you look at it. Make sure the property has equity. If the seller tells you it's owned, free and clear, or it has a low mortgage relative to the ARV, you've struck gold! If the property has little to no equity, but will cash flow (rents exceed all expenses and debt service), you can wholesale this property as a lease option or keep it as a lease option for yourself. Never discuss an offer price until you have had the chance to actually view the property. Also, many sellers will not take your offer seriously until you have seen it because they believe it is impossible to make a real evaluation on the property without seeing it. Go to the appendix to view the 100 Percent Financed Motivated Seller Script. Contact the motivated seller back if their property fits your business model.

2. **Research property (at home) to verify who owns the property, whether or not it has been listed before, and the approximate ARV.** ARV deals with the value of the investment property after the renovation is complete. This number is determined by getting an appraisal, taking into account the construction budget and comparable houses in the neighborhood. Typically, recently renovated homes have the higher price points. These property prices will give you the ARV. The lower prices of recently sold comparable properties (comps) are the properties that have not been updated (wholesale prices). These wholesale prices will help you determine the price to pay when buying a property to wholesale out to an end buyer, such as a rehabilitator or buy and hold investor.

Residential property prices are based on the prices of comps that have sold recently in an area. Comps are properties that have the same square footage within (400 sq. ft. of the subject property), the same number of baths and bedrooms, and are within 10 years old of the subject property.

## Comp Checklist

✓ Same bathroom count

✓ Same bedroom count

✓ Within 400 sq. feet of the subject property

✓ Built within 10 years of the subject property

✓ Sold within the last 90 days

Only one property is necessary; however, the more properties you can find that match the above criteria, the better.

## Example Subject Property:

– 3 beds

– 2 baths

– 1,500 sq. feet

– Built in 1968

– Brick

Today's date: 6/3/2016

## *Comparable properties*

*Within 1-2 miles in most cases*

### **COMP 1:**
- 3 beds
- 2 baths
- 1,300 sq. feet
- Built in 1965
- Brick front
- Same neighborhood

Recently sold for $200,000

Sold: 5/14/2016

### **COMP 2:**
- 3 beds
- 1.5 baths
- 1,600 sq. ft.
- Built in 1973
- Brick

*(Two houses down the street from the subject property)*

Recently sold for $209,000

Sold: 6/1/2016

## COMP 3:
- 3 beds
- 2 baths
- 1,200 sq. ft.
- Built in 1966
- Frame

*(Three blocks away from the subject property)*

Recently sold for $210,000

Sold: 5/28/2016

## NON-COMP 1:
- 4 beds
- 2 baths
- 2,000 sq. feet
- Built in 1965
- Brick front
- Same neighborhood

Recently sold for $173,000

Sold: 5/07/2016

## NON-COMP 2:

- 2 beds
- 1.5 baths
- 1,000 sq. ft.
- Built in 1983
- Frame

*(Two houses down the street from the subject property)*

Recently sold for $100,000

Sold: 2/12/2016


## NON-COMP 3:

- 2 beds
- 2 baths
- 11,000 sq. ft.
- Built in 1996
- Brick front

*(Three blocks away from subject property)*

Recently sold for $230,000

Sold: 5/14/2016

If you look at the comps vs. the non-comps, you notice the average prices for the comps in the area are approximately $208,000. The non-comps' recently sold prices do not matter because those properties are not comps. If the offer price is 65% of ARV or lower with minimal repairs, this may be a deal you want to look into further.

3. **Set up an appointment to view the property** if the details of the script are good, and it fits your business model.

4. **Go to the property to build rapport with the motivated sellers, and estimate necessary repairs.** Build rapport by complimenting them on something and find something you have in common with them (kids, gardening, sports teams).

When you meet the seller, build rapport and figure out why they need to sell. If a seller is not motivated, the seller will not be ready for an investor's offer. Sellers give clues of their motivation when you meet them. Some of them like to talk for hours, but some of them like to talk about everything but the property. Others barely say a word. The sellers who are quiet are the hardest to build rapport with. The better you become at being someone they can respect, the more deals you will close. Showing compassion for a seller's tough situation may mean the world to them. Again, some sellers are motivated as a result of divorce, death, loss of job, and/or foreclosure. Do your best to ease their frustrations. As you speak with people, pay attention to what they say about their situation as well as the property. After talking with the sellers, record a quick video of the interior and exterior of the house. You can use a smartphone. If you don't have a smartphone, a digital camera will do. Your buyers want to see pictures of the actual home.

After you finish talking with the motivated seller, take pictures of the interior and exterior of the property. Estimating repairs is a lot easier than you may believe. Repair estimates vary with each property and will ultimately be the decision of the end buyer. The end buyer needs to do his or her own due diligence. As a wholesaler, keep your focus on what makes you the most money, which is finding fixer uppers for buyers, not doing an in-depth analysis of what repairs are needed. As you develop a buyers list, you will quickly find that each buyer has his/her own criteria and cost matrix for properties they acquire. I have some buyers that totally remodel homes, while others try to spend as little as possible on the rehab. To differentiate yourself from a realtor, eyeball the property and take note of things that need repair. Provide that list to your buyer and let them determine rehab estimate. You can also find an investor-friendly contractor to provide a rehab estimate. Look at projects the investor-contractor is currently working on, and ask him to tell you the cost of everything. A lot of times, they use price per square foot to measure painting and carpet. You can view similar houses you are going to wholesale with the investor-friendly contractors to get an idea of the repair costs. A quick estimate formula is below.

## The Quick Estimate Formula:

$7-$9 x square footage of the subject property - (rental property)

$10-$12 x square footage of the subject property - (fix and flip to retail buyer)

$13-$15 (or higher) x square footage of the subject property (high-end flips)

### EXAMPLE 1:

1,200 sq. ft. house in okay condition (high rental area)

(In need of minor fixes: paint, carpet and updated appliances)

1,200 sq. ft. x $9 = $10,800 in repairs, give or take a few thousand dollars

**EXAMPLE 2:**

1,800 sq. ft. house in poor condition (homeowner area)

(Needs to be gutted down to the studs)

1,800 sq. ft. x $12 = $21,000 in repairs. If it needs major repair, I would add a few thousand dollars to the amount.

**EXAMPLE 3:**

3,000 sq. ft. house in poor condition (high-end area)

(Go with all high-end finishes)

3,000 sq. ft. x $15 = $45,000 in repairs

This is just an estimate. The buyer will pay for the repairs. Always tell your buyers to do their own due diligence and repair estimates. This is a very slippery slope. If you underestimate or overestimate the repairs, your buyer may walk. Maintain control by letting them assess the property after you place it under contract.

5. **Leave the property and tell the motivated seller you will do your due diligence** and present an offer within 24 hours. Enter the subject property's address into www.zillow.com and

http://www.totalviewrealestate.com/index.php to find out additional information about the property. Both sites are great for getting quick comps and determining a snapshot ARV. Go to the county tax assessor's website to find out whose name is on the title of the property, how long the sellers owned the property, and how much the sellers paid for the property. Do the math and come up with your Maximum Allowable Offer (MAO).

Determining how much you should offer motivated sellers to buy their house is critical. Never offer more than your MAO.

## MAO Formula:

> ARV x .65 - (Estimated Repairs) - (Your Profit) = MAO

For example, let's say the ARV is $100,000, the estimated repairs are $20,000, and you want to make $5,000 on the deal.

**Your MAO will be:**

ARV = $100,000

Repairs = $20,000

Profit = $5,000

> $100,000 (ARV) x .65 - $20,000 (Repairs) - $5,000 (Profit) = $40,000

In this case, your MAO will be $40,000 to your seller.

Most of the properties you come across will not work. Sometimes, the seller doesn't want to take a low price. Sometimes, the buyer is not willing to pay a higher price or the numbers simply don't work. Wholesaling is a numbers game, and this is part of the process. Do not stop! Just keep going!

6. **After you determine the MAO**, reconnect with the seller to present the offer. If the property is free and clear, present three offers:

   ✓ *Option 1:* All cash

   ✓ *Option 2:* Some cash now

   ✓ *Option 3:* Some cash later and monthly payments

Options 2 and 3 are owner-financed deals that you can pitch to other investors, just in case the seller rejects your cash offer. Let the seller know what you intend to offer and send it via email. If you read other books or training materials, they may recommend you go back out to present the offer in person. However, if you have built enough rapport with the seller in your prior meeting, a phone call will do. If you have not built enough rapport, the face-to-face visit may make a huge difference. If you're not a little uncomfortable when presenting your offer to the seller, you probably have not gone low enough.

Sellers always have a higher number in their heads of what a property is worth. Most sellers believe their property is worth a lot more because they value it differently than an investor. At times, the motivated sellers have an emotional attachment to the home. Buyers, who are also investors, place value solely in the numbers; they do not have an emotional attachment to the property. Motivated sellers place value on a lot of things that have nothing to do with the actual value of the property. Motivated sellers will listen and respond to your offer, as long as it makes sense to them.

Don't worry if the sellers get offended by your low offer. If they are really motivated, they will present a counteroffer. You have to make sure the numbers work for you and your potential end buyer. If that means cutting your profit from $5,000 to $3,500 so this deal will work, so be it. Some motivated sellers will shut down; some will accept, and some will want to think their decision over. This is why establishing rapport, and reminding them that your offer is the best price you can come up with that's also beneficial to them. Do not worry if the sellers are not willing to accept your MAO now. A "No" doesn't always mean no. Consider it to be a "not yet, but give us time." As a wholesaler, having patience and following up weekly is key to your success. Some sellers will shop around and try to get a better price in the market. Sellers need a dose of reality when it comes to valuations of their properties. They need to realize, through shopping around, that your numbers are better and that they will end up working with you later down the line anyway. If not, proceed to the next one. There is always another deal out there with your name on it.

7. **The motivated seller accepted your offer, now get it under contract.** There needs to be a legally binding agreement between you and the motivated sellers of property. This agreement is usually a Purchase and Sale Agreement, or a Purchase Option Agreement. A Purchase and Sale Agreement is a legal document that defines the property address, asking price, deposit information, closing date and closing attorney information. This document locks both you and the seller into an agreement, stating that you will purchase the property by a specified date and the

seller cannot sell the property to another party that is not designated by you. This document becomes binding once you give the seller a deposit and both parties have signed the agreement. Deposits are also referred to as consideration. Once a Purchase and Sale Agreement is signed, the seller cannot sell the property to anyone else. The buyer has to purchase the property within the inspection period or you will lose your deposit. If the sellers do not fulfill their end of the deal, you can take legal action against them for damages.

With a Purchase Option Agreement, the buyer has the right (option) to purchase the property for a certain price by a specified date, but does not have to purchase it. With purchase options, the seller has the right to sell the property to another party or hold onto it if they choose. There is no deposit (option) money transferred. Purchase and Sale Agreements can be daunting and filled with clauses and addendums, which is typically what scares a lot of wholesalers away. Most states have a standard contract most realtors use. These agreements are usually filled with verbiage to protect both the buyer and seller. You can find an investor-friendly attorney to draft a Purchase and Sale Agreement for you. Tell the buyer and the seller that you will need to use your forms and closing attorney on your deals.

Sometimes, you will have to compromise to make deals work, but stick to your guns generally. Not all attorneys and real estate agents are used to working with wholesalers. These people can kill your deals because they may not understand what you are doing. To minimize this, use your investor-friendly closing attorney and recommended paperwork. If the seller is motivated (like they are supposed to be), they will not have an issue with this.

8. **After the contract is signed, contact your closing attorney's title company.** If you already had a buyers' list (or know other wholesalers who do), email the details of this wholesale deal to them. If you do not have a buyers' list, learn how to build one. Closing attorneys and title companies are easy to contact. The easiest way to find a closing attorney is by doing a Google search in your local vicinity. You can find tons of them online. Contact other investors and real estate professionals in your real estate network and ask for their recommendations.

Connect with investor-friendly title companies and closing attorneys. If they are not investor-friendly, they may tell you what you can't do or that some things you want to do are illegal. When this happens, kindly thank them for their time and move on to the next one on your list. Depending on what state you live in, you will either close with a title company or a closing attorney. Make sure all of the paperwork is correct and properly recorded in the state and county records. Closing attorneys are paid a fee to process this paperwork. Closing fees can be costly, depending on who you're working with. These entities are vital in every real estate closing, so choose wisely. Go to https://sandygadow.com/state-by-state-closing-guide/ to find out if you live in a title state or closing attorney state. If this does not help you, reach out to a realtor in your area for more clarification.

The webpage below may help you determine whom you will work with. Reach out to a few of them and find out who will process your transactions. Make sure you introduce yourself and let them know you are a real estate investor. http://www.owners.com /fsbo-articles/title-and-escrow/choosing-a-title-company-escrow-officer-or-real-estate-attorney. Here is a simple script you can use:

*"Hi my name is (Your Name). I am a real estate investor new to the (your city/target market) market, and I am interested in working with (name of title company or closing attorney). I have three quick questions for you:*

1. *Do you work with investors?*

2. *Can you process a double closing and/or Assignment of Contract?*

3. *Do you have any available properties that you need to liquidate?"*

If they answer *yes* to the third question, make sure you get the address and the asking price. Find ten title companies in your area, and write down their numbers. Call them right away. If you are serious about becoming a wholesaler, this will not be a problem for you. You *must* take action to be successful. You can write the information in the following chart for future reference.

| Company Name | Phone | Website URL |
| --- | --- | --- |
|  |  |  |
|  |  |  |
|  |  |  |
|  |  |  |
|  |  |  |
|  |  |  |
|  |  |  |
|  |  |  |
|  |  |  |
|  |  |  |
|  |  |  |
|  |  |  |
|  |  |  |
|  |  |  |
|  |  |  |
|  |  |  |
|  |  |  |
|  |  |  |
|  |  |  |
|  |  |  |
|  |  |  |
|  |  |  |

Once you find an attorney you are comfortable with, submit the Purchase and Sale Agreement to the title company/closing attorney to get the title search started. During this process, the title company/closing attorney will look at the property records to make sure there is nothing to hinder the sale of the property. If there is something like a mortgage, tax claim, or another party listed on the title, this is considered a "clouded title." If a property has a clouded title, the property cannot be sold until the issue has been resolved. If there is a mortgage listed, it must be paid in full or released by the bank. If there is a tax claim on the property that has not been paid, it must be paid in full, and the seller will keep the remaining balance. If there is another party listed as an owner of the property, they must be notified and will have to approve the transaction (if not deceased). The reputation and licenses of these title companies are at stake, so they make sure they get these things processed correctly. This takes pressure off your back when dealing with fussy sellers or buyers. Once you have a property under contract with a buyer and seller, and if there are any issues regarding closing, refer them to your attorney or title company.

9. **Now it's time to assign your contract to a qualified buyer.** If you do not have any buyers, I will show you how to build a list. You can always email your wholesale deal to other wholesalers to see if they have a qualified buyer, but you will have to split the assignment fee with them.

## *You are almost to the money!*

Once you have a contract in hand and you've submitted it to the closing attorney/title company, the next step is to find a buyer. Some would argue that you need to build a buyers list first. This is an excellent way to start. But, going after motivated sellers first will force you to find buyers. Either way is acceptable, but you do not want to attract buyers if you don't have deals readily available to email them. Finding buyers is actually pretty easy in any market. Buyers are abundant, even though the nightly news paints a different story. There are many real estate entrepreneurs who buy and sell properties daily. In fact, I'm one of them and I love purchasing properties from wholesalers. These buyers have the resources to purchase properties *all cash*. As the saying goes, "Cash is king," and this definitely rings true for real estate.

# TOP THREE WAYS TO FIND BUYERS:

1. Bandit Signs
2. Realtors
3. Networking for buy and hold investors, flippers, and other wholesalers at REIA groups

You may have to share your assignment fee if you use another wholesaler's buyer.

## *Bandit Signs*

One of the best ways to locate buyers is through the use of bandit signs. They can be used to attract buyers and sellers. You should always position your bandit signs in two areas:

1. Your target property zip code
2. Zip codes where the population has more discretionary income

Placing "Nice 3/2 Handyman Special for Sale" or "We Buy Ugly Houses Fast with Cash" bandit signs in more upscale communities is a good idea because these communities tend to have a higher median income. Most buyers who are looking for deals will read your bandit sign and contact you through your Google Voice number. Even if you don't have properties for sale, put the signs up anyway. If a buyer calls, let him/her know the property is no longer available and follow the script below:

*"Hi, my name is (your name). I am a real estate wholesaler in the (your city/target market). Thanks for reaching out. Can you tell me a little more about the areas you like to purchase in and the types of properties you purchase? More specifically, what are your target zip codes, the number of bedrooms and baths, construction type, age, and price range?"*

As you speak with the buyer, find out their interests and life outside of work. Listen intently. After all, we are all humans, and we like to work with people we trust and respect. Again, establishing credibility is a must! After you get an idea of what kind of property the buyer is looking for, you may want to ask additional questions.

Asking, "How fast can you close?" lets you know the buyer's intentions. A time frame of 30 days or longer is usually a sign of another wholesaler. Working with other wholesalers is an excellent way to close more deals. But you don't want another wholesaler to lock down your property. Get it under contract first before you share the details of your deal with another wholesaler. If you are having trouble finding a buyer, working with another wholesaler is a great way to close a deal. You just need to know how the buyer plans to close. The fewer parties involved in your transactions, the more profitable it will be for you.

Asking, "Are you using cash, financing, or hard money?" gives you an idea of how fast a buyer can close. According to Wikipedia, a hard money loan is a specific type of asset-based loan financing through which a borrower receives funds secured by real property. Hard money loans are typically issued by private investors or companies. Cash can be considered savings, retirement accounts, or any other funds you're coming out of pocket to finance the costs; you're not working with private investors or companies.

Cash closers are quicker and rarely give you issues. Hard money lenders are fast as well, but the loans have to be approved by the hard moneylender. Sometimes, the lender will not approve a loan, and the buyer will walk away. If a buyer walks, your potential deal and payment can be delayed or disappear entirely if you cannot replace a buyer for the particular property before your seller contract runs out.

In most cases, financing will not work because a conventional lender may not want to offer a loan on a property that needs extensive repairs. Most of the properties that wholesalers deal with need extensive repairs. Financing also takes a lot more time. Banks can take up to 120 days or longer to approve a loan.

Asking, "When was your last closing?" tells you about the frequency of the buyer's purchasing process.

Asking, "Will you be the end buyer, or do you plan to assign the contract?" is a critical question. Make sure you are dealing with a cash buyer, not a tire kicker or another wholesaler who is trying to lock down your property. Working with other wholesalers can be quite lucrative, but you don't want to give up control of a contract to another party. If the wholesaler actually has a buyer lined up, it can be a great situation. But if not, keep in touch with the wholesaler, and go find another buyer.

Asking, "Which closing attorney do you use?" gives you a clear picture of where and how they close their deals. If they work with an attorney you are familiar with, it gives you the chance to build more rapport. On the other hand, if they use an attorney you haven't worked with, use this opportunity to expand your network. Either way, it's a win-win situation. Answers to these questions will give you an idea of the kind of buyer you are dealing with. Most real buyers won't have an issue with these questions, especially if you have built rapport. If the buyer has difficulty answering any of these questions, they may be wasting your time.

## Working with Realtors

Another great way to find cash buyers is to connect with a realtor or broker. Working with realtors has many benefits. Realtors can pull comparable properties from the MLS and send you properties, based on criteria you specify. When you reach out to a realtor, let them know you are an investor and the types of properties you desire. Expired listings also serve as a great resource.

When finding buyers, have the realtor look up all cash transactions in the city. When you analyze the list, you will quickly see which zip codes have the most cash transactions. Once you find the zip codes, you will have an idea of where buyers are buying the most. With this information, contact buyers by searching the property tax records. It's not difficult to find buyer information, especially if the buyer is an institutional buyer. If you see the same name in the tax records repeatedly for different properties, this typically means you have found a landlord or an institutional buyer. Most of the time, a good realtor can find buyer information for you. Once you find the contact information for a potential buyer, reach out to them and inform them of your services and the properties you have available.

## Real Estate Networking Events

The last strategy we will discuss when looking to connect with buyers is to attend your local Real Estate Investors Association (REIA) meetings. Real estate investors host these meetings for other real estate investors. Typically, you can join for a one-time fee, or pay for each meeting you attend.

Listen to speakers and take notes. Let them know about your services. The key is to network.

Let everyone you encounter know what you do, and let them know what properties you have available for wholesale. If you find an investor or flipper, let them know you are a wholesaler. Use your time wisely at the meetings by making connections with buyers, sellers and other wholesalers.

# LOCKING DOWN A CONTRACT WITH YOUR BUYER

Now, you have to get your buyer to commit to purchasing your property. After you assign your contract to the buyer, make sure the transaction moves smoothly until the end. Then, you show up at the closing table and receive your assignment fee check. Money is always exchanged at the closing table. You get your assignment fee check from the settlement company if your assignment fee is listed on the HUD statement. Keep in mind that I am not an attorney. It is best to set up an LLC that is strictly for wholesaling, and have your checks made out to that entity. However, always cover your assets and consult your attorney. Each state has different real estate laws, so it's smart to get an attorney's advice first. Wholesaling is a business, so establishing a business checking account to deposit your profits is recommended.

Louis from upstate New York applied these principles under the tutelage of this book, and his first closed deal generated a profit of $16,000! This one deal took him almost eight months to close because he had issues with the seller. Keep in mind, Louis didn't work 40 hours a week for eight months to make $16,000; he worked on average four hours per week. So, if he worked four hours per week x 32 weeks, it took him 128 hours to generate $16,000. He made $125/hour on average. That's good money, considering Louis didn't bring his credit or cash into the equation.

After you close on a wholesale deal, share your success with all private lenders or partners. Share your success stories so you can establish credibility. Eventually, you may whet their appetite enough for them to inquire about partnering with you for your buy and hold strategy. Do not live off your wholesale profits. Wholesaling is a means to an end; it's not the end. Wholesaling is comparable to a part-time job. Use your wholesale profits to save for down payments, repair your credit, pay down debt, and improve your DTC ratio. This is your ticket to financial freedom.

Once you get the hang of wholesaling, you'll have the mindset of an investor. Then, when your financial situation improves to the point you can start buying and holding properties, you'll be in a great position. You'll be able to pick the best deals for your buy and hold strategy, and wholesale the less profitable deals to other end buyers.

Again, your goal is to obtain mailbox money from your passive income. You don't want to send direct mail to someone's mailbox forever.

 **KEY PRINCIPLES**

- **Be persistent.** Devote at least 20 hours a week to your wholesale business, networking and learning.

- **Don't just take our advice, but the advice of other wholesalers in your local market who are successful.**

- **People who have an abundance mentality will be open to sharing knowledge.** All you have to do is ask!

- **Wholesaling is a numbers game, so you may have to send out a thousand direct mail pieces to generate a few calls.** Out of the few, one or two may be qualified leads. You only have to close one.

- **Aim for one wholesale deal per month, and use the proceeds to improve your credit and save for down payments.** You will be ready to buy and hold for passive profits.

# Wash, Rinse & Repeat

Now that you know what to do, you must be consistent. As an entrepreneur, you need continual access to the deals and the money. Work to improve your financial situation in order to qualify for mortgages and business credit. Reach out to more deal finders. Wholesale until you improve your credit and acquire enough out-of-pocket cash. Network to find investors who may want to partner with you on your next deal.

Every time you close a deal, update your financial freedom goal on your personal financial statement. The number of units in your portfolio is not that important. The amount of cash flow you receive each month is more important. Once you achieve your financial freedom goal, and have six months' living expenses in the bank, do a property inspection on all properties before you quit your job. That way, you will not have any unpleasant surprises. Then, submit your resignation letter and two weeks' notice.

After you quit your job, continue to improve your properties by doing necessary repairs. Increase your rent, add coined laundry, contest taxes, reduce your insurance payment, install water conservation kits if you pay water and pay off high debt. Focus on improving the revenue of every property you own, as well as decreasing your expenses and debt service annually.

If you start a new business (wholesaling or flipping real estate, for example) after quitting your job, use the profits from the business to invest in more real estate, to pay off debt, or to make necessary repairs. It's important to reinvest your business earnings. Invest it in the strategy that produces the highest cash-on-cash return.

For instance, imagine you have $20,000 in profits from your new business. Instead of having fun with the money, reinvest it. Here are your options: You closed on a deal some months ago using business credit. You have a business credit card with a $20,000 balance, in which you had a minimum payment of $400 per month. If you pay off a business credit card with that $20,000 you received in profits from your business, your cash-on-cash return would be ($400 x 12 months)/$20,000 = 24%. However, if you found a duplex that cash flowed $300 per month that requires $20,000 out of your pocket to close the deal, your cash-on-cash return would be ($300 x 12 months)/$20,000 = 18%. When you do the cash-on-cash return analysis, it makes financial sense to use that $20,000 to pay off the business credit card. You will have a higher cash-on-cash return and make an additional $400 a month in cash flow since you no longer have to make that minimum payment toward your business credit card. Again, the philosophy is to buy the chicken so you can only eat the eggs. If you get access to additional funds, always look for the next chicken (deal) who will lay eggs (passive income).

Not only do you need to update your income statement and financial freedom goal, but you also need to update your balance sheet. Monitor your chickens to see how fat they have become (equity).

If the equity grows to 20% for a particular property, reach out to a mortgage broker for a cash-out refinance. Use that equity to either pay off debt or to roll the proceeds into your next deal. There is a natural progression of a real estate investor. You may start off buying a duplex in year one, a single-family in year two, a six-unit in year three, and two ten-units in year four. Continue to grow and stretch yourself each year; continue to play a bigger game and don't become complacent.

## WEIGH THE ADVICE YOU RECEIVE

Be mindful of who mentors you. Screen them wisely. If they are not living the lifestyle you desire to live, not actively investing in real estate, or if they don't have a considerably larger portfolio than you, don't accept advice from them. They may provide advice contrary to the ideas covered in this book. Real estate agents, attorneys and mortgage lenders may provide you with contrary advice, as well. Weigh the advice you receive. Find local real estate investors in the markets you're interested in holding properties, and interview them. You are an entrepreneur, so you have to make that executive decision. The ball is in your court.

If you'd like to follow our proven system and utilize our trusted services with our reputable team, see the 100PF Appendix. We'd love to offer our services to help you become one of the 100,000 early retirees.

This book may be new content for you, a new way of thinking. Study this book at least five times. Brainwash yourself into success. These things need to sink deep into your subconscious mind, to the point you believe you are a successful, full-time real estate investor, even though you may be broke with bad credit today. Free yourself from stinking thinking. Wash, rinse and repeat.

Your most dominant thought will always become your reality. If you do not have an abundance of positive thoughts about money in your brain, you won't have an abundance of positive cash flow in your bank. To make sure you have the right thoughts, I want you to say these affirmations listed below, day in and day out, until you have an abundance of cash flow—enough to quit your job. Say them with feeling and passion. Imagine yourself doing the things listed in these affirmations as you recite them. Get excited! Get pumped! Imagine your friends and partners congratulating you on your success. Perform this mental exercise every time you recite these affirmations.

# DAILY AFFIRMATIONS
*(recite twice a day)*

1. I am highly ambitious. I am a multimillionaire.
2. I am cool, calm and collected. I'm my own boss; I am debonair.
3. Money comes to me easily and frequently.
4. God continues to bless me, exceedingly and repeatedly.
5. I live the life that I love. I love the life that I live.
6. I dominate this real estate investing game since I am a financial wiz.
7. I have all the money, all the credit, all the resources for my business that I need.
8. I am the definition of what a successful real estate entrepreneur looks like.
9. I keep my goals high, and I aim for the fences.
10. My passive income far outweighs my living expenses.
11. I do not need a 9-to-5 because I have achieved my financial independence.
12. I walk by faith and not by sight. I am not a slave to my senses.
13. If I believe it, I can achieve it.

14. As long as I conceive it, I will receive it. Please believe it!
15. Day by day, I am getting better.
16. It felt good to turn in my resignation letter.
17. When I get undesirable results, I find it funny.
18. I receive, "Wake up whenever I feel like it" money.
19. I am as tenacious as a bulldog, lockjaw.
20. I will not stop pursuing my dreams until I am the top dog.
21. I love my life, and I am so happy to be me.
22. It feels great to wake up every morning and be financially free.

Even though you may read this book a hundred times, and recite the above affirmations with feeling a thousand times, you may see results contrary to your desires. You may get rejected. You may receive denial letters from mortgage lenders in the mail. You may have several people refuse to work with you. Unexpected bills may come. Unexpected repairs will arise. Contractors may screw you over. Tenants may destroy your property. You may have to chase tenants for rent. Deals will fall through. You may lose money. All these things happened to me. But, I survived it. You will, too.

The hardest labor in the world is mental labor. Mental labor is believing you are a successful real estate entrepreneur, despite your bad credit and lack of money. It is believing you are financially free and independent, despite the fact that you lack knowledge to properly structure deals in the beginning. It is believing you are prosperous, despite the mountain of bills sitting on your dining room table. It is believing you are successful, despite all the failures you faced. Only a small number of people can think positive in the sea of negativity. They control their minds to think one way, and one way only, despite the negative circumstances that happen all around them. That is why so few are successful.

It is hard labor to think positively, to stay focused on your desires, to control your emotions, and selectively ignore those undesirable circumstances. It's hard work, but you must be a steward over your thought life and emotions. If you experience an undesirable circumstance, use that as a sign to reread your creed, resignation letter and affirmations. Your day job is a means to an end, but not the end. While working your 9-to-5, do your best—but give your all to your real estate investing business. This book serves as a real estate investor's blueprint to success, but you have to maintain that burning desire. If you do not have a burning desire, you will quit when things get difficult. If you do not have a burning desire, you will move on to something else when you don't see immediate results. If you don't have a burning desire, you will never become a full-time real estate investor.

I have gained much more success since I quit my job. My job helped me qualify for mortgages and put food on the table, but it hindered me from pursuing my purpose in life. If you do not pursue your true purpose, you are robbing society of your gifts. Not only that, you are robbing yourself of success. Lastly, you are occupying a position at your job that someone else needs to fill. Don't quit hustling until you obtain your financial freedom goal.

I believe you'll be highly successful, why, because I believe in you. I believe you can do it. You didn't pick up this book by chance. It was meant for you to read it. Make sure you take all of these words to heart and apply them daily. Take action! The road to financial freedom may be a rocky one, filled with uncertainty. Use this book as your guide. 100 Percent Financed wants to be your guide to financial freedom. Stay connected with us on all our social media platforms:

1. Website: www.100percentfinanced.com

2. YouTube: 100 Percent Financed

3. Instagram: 100percentfinanced

4. Facebook: www.facebook.com/100percentfinanced

5. Blog: 100percentfinanced.com

 **KEY PRINCIPLES**

- **There is always a silver lining.** Search for it.

- **It's important to know your numbers.**

- **Play a bigger game.** Don't be afraid to seek bigger deals. The only difference between a two-unit and a 20-unit is a 0. The process is the same.

- **Stay positive.** I have never met a successful person who did not maintain a positive outlook on life.

- **Do not be fazed by life's circumstances.** You are the master of your fate. You can alter your future and change your circumstances, as long as you alter your mindset. You are an entrepreneur. Make it happen.

- **Brainwash yourself into success.** Reread this content at least five times. Recite the creed, resignation letter, and affirmations twice a day religiously. No excuses!

> Beloved, I wish above all things that thou mayest prosper and be in health, even as thy soul prospereth.
>
> –3 John 1:2 (KJV)

*May God bless you the cost of this book, one hundred thousand times over!*

*Earn Passively, Live Passionately!*

*To Your Success,*

As mentioned in the special thanks, I wouldn't be where I am today if it hadn't been for my Lord Jesus Christ. I'm a firm believer in having not only financial wealth but physical, mental and spiritual wealth. If you're interested in having a relationship with Jesus Christ as you grow in wealth, and according to Romans 10:9-10: *"That if thou shalt confess with thy mouth the Lord Jesus, and shalt believe in thine heart that God hath raised him from the dead, thou shalt be saved. For with the heart man believeth unto righteousness; and with the mouth confession is made unto salvation."*

# 100PF SERVICES
## Appendix

**Business credit:**
https://www.100percentfinanced.com/business-credit-cards

**Multiunit Acquisition Program:**
https://www.100percentfinanced.com/multi-unit-acquisition-program

**Share Hub:**
https://www.100percentfinanced.com/content-hub

**Blog:**
https://www.100percentfinanced.com/blog

**Youtube Channel:**
https://www.youtube.com/channel/UC6Pl8TV9HQI2PGXaEciWSgw

**Instagram:**
https://www.instagram.com/100percentfinanced/

**Real Estate Coaching:**
https://www.100percentfinanced.com/multi-unitaquisition

**Credit Repair:**
https://www.100percentfinanced.com/credit-repair-5

*For other services not listed in this book, go to*
100percenttfinanced.com

# WHOLESALING
# Appendix

Sample Direct Mail <https://drive.google.com/file/d/0By- U5XKEd0SsM2k5NzBBRmxVVk0/edit>. Feel free to edit it to your specifications.

## 100 Percent Financed Sample Direct Mail for Motivated Sellers

Hi Motivated Seller,

My name is Wholesaler. I am a real estate investor and I would like to $$ BUY $$ your house at ★★★★★★★★★★★★★★★★★★ Drive.

Please call me at xxx.xxx.xxxx.

I can make you a cash offer and close FAST – in less than 30 days! There is no obligation. Please give me a call to discuss.

Thanks!

*—Wholesaler*

Dear {homeowner},

My name is Wholesaler. My wife is Wholesalia. We'd like to buy your house at {property address}.

Please call me at 555-555-1234.

Thanks,

*—Wholesaler*

---

**Postcard or repeated attempts:**

I have been desperately trying to reach you for a few months now in reference to your property located at _____. I have tried just about everything to get in contact with you, unsuccessfully. So, I'm sending you this postcard. My partner and I buy 5-6 houses a month, and we are very interested in buying your property ASAP! We are CASH buyers and we can settle in two weeks. We have a team of general contractors who are ready to begin work as soon as possible, so if the property needs work, not a problem. Please call me back as soon as you receive this postcard so that we can buy your property immediately.

*Mr. Wholesaler*
123-555-1234
iwillbuyyouruglyhouseinaheartbeat@gmail.com
www.iwillbuyyouruglyhouseinaheartbeat.com

## Sample ads to attract sellers:

- ✓ Cash for your home in 24 hours! (Your Number)
- ✓ We buy homes for Cash - (Your Number)
- ✓ (Your name) will buy your Home today for cash.
- ✓ Give us a Call at (Your Number) Or I Will Make An Offer On Your Home Today!
- ✓ Call Mike (Your Number) Sell Today! I pay cash for homes.
- ✓ Call YOUR NAME - (Your Number) Behind In Payments? I can fix it for you!
- ✓ Call YOUR NAME - (Your Number) I Pay FULL Market Value! For Real Estate!
- ✓ (Your Number) (Alphabetical Listing If This Is How Your Newspaper Lists Their Classifieds) A Guaranteed Offer on Your Home In 24 Hrs! Call (Your Number) ALL CASH! For Your Home (Your Number) FREE REPORT Sell Your Home In 24 HOURS! (Your Number) recording http://www.ATLANTA_ALLCashBuyer.com FREE REPORT We Will Pay CASH For Your Home! (Your Number) recording http://www.ATLANTA_ALLCashBuyer.com FREE REPORT How to Sell a Problem Property! (Your Number) recording http://www.ATLANTA_ALLCashBuyer.com

## My Craigslist.com and backpage.com Seller ad

✓ Don't Panic! I WILL BUY YOUR HOUSE ALL CASH FAST! (Atlanta Metroplex)

www.abcbuyyourhousefastandinahurry.com We specialize in helping people who need to sell their house quickly for a variety of circumstances. Some of the reasons we see most often are: - Behind on payments or facing foreclosure - Recently divorced - Transferring Jobs or relocating - Bought a new property and need to sell the old one now - Need to settle an Estate - Real Estate agent couldn't sell the house - Tired of being a landlord - House is vacant and costs are piling up - House needs extensive repairs

www.abcbuyyourhousefastandinahurry.com Why work with us? - Guaranteed property sale at competitive, agreed upon price - Fast and hassle free, offer in 48 hours or less - We use private funding so we can close in 7-14 days or less - We handles all the paperwork and make all of the arrangements - You will get a simple, no hassle closing with NO cost to you - Property purchased "As-Is" with no further expense, clean up, repairs or improvements - No Realtors fees or commissions. We don't want to list your house, we Buy it all Cash! - Strict confidentiality - WE BUY YOUR HOUSE ALL CASH! Contact us now for more information on how you can get started today 24-hour hotline. Call 123-555-1234, or email: abcbuyyourhousefastandinahurry@gmail.com, or visit our website at: www.abcbuyyourhousefastandinahurry.com

---

**Sample Ad to Attract Buyers:**

I have always received a good response with: I Have 3 houses MUST Sell ALL Plz Call: (Your Buyer Phone line) Must Sell Now Cheap Cash (Your Buyer Phone line) Motivated Seller Cheap Cash (Your Buyer Phone line) Desperate Seller Cheap Cash (Your Buyer Phone line) Hard Times Must Sell (Your Buyer Phone line) Handyman Specials Cheap Cash (Your Buyer Phone line) Fixer-Upper Homes Cheap Cash (Your Buyer Phone line) Place ads online on craigslist, backpage, kijiji etc. Got Cash? We have deep discounted properties for sale Visit our website at http://www.abcdbuyahouseatlantaganow.com Got Cash? We have cheap wholesale deals for you Visit our website at abcdbuyahouseatlantaganow.com

---

## 100 Percent Financed Motivated Seller Script

*Thank you for all the information you provided. Mr. (wholesaler name) will be back in the office tomorrow and I will make sure he receives the information about your home. Someone will contact you about setting up a time for him or myself to come out and view the property.*

---

## Phone Script:

*Hello, this is (wholesaler name) office. Are you calling to sell your house, buy a house, or for some other matter?*

---

## Selling

*Option #1 Script for Motivated Home Owners Calling to Sell:*

✓ Can I please have your name?

_____
_____

✓ What is the address of the property?

_____
_____

✓ What is the best contact phone number for you?

_____

_____

✓ Do you own the home alone or does someone else own it with you?

_____

_____

✓ Do you live in the home? Is it rented, or vacant?

_____

_____

✓ How many bedrooms does the house have?

_____

✓ How many baths are in your home?

_____

✓ What is the approximate square footage of your home? _____

✓ Does your home have a garage?

_____

✓ How long have you owned the home?

_____

✓ Why are you selling?

_____

_____

_____

_____

✓ How much do you owe on the property?

_____

_____

✓ What is the monthly payment on the property?

_____

_____

✓ Are you behind on your payments? If so, by how much? _____

_____

✓ How much would your house rent for?

_____

_____

✓ Can you tell me how much the property taxes, insurance and HOA fees are for the property?

Taxes _____

Insurance _____

HOA Fees _____

✓ Does the property need any repairs? If so, what's needed? _____

_____

_____

_____

_____

# Glossary

**100 Percent Financed:** Obtaining an income-producing asset, using little to none of your money. You are financing the asset 100%.

**Acquisition Fee:** Closing costs and commission fees one pays for the purchase of a property.

**Affirmation:** Positive statements continually repeated until they become a reality.

**After Repair Value (ARV):** The appraised value of the asset after all repairs are made.

**Appraisal:** An expert assessment of the value of real property.

**Appreciation:** An increase in the value of an asset over time. The increase can occur for a number of reasons, including how well you manage the asset (forced appreciation), a result of changes in inflation or increase in interest rates.

**Asset:** Property owned by a person or company regarded as having value

**Assignment Fee:** The money a wholesaler is paid from a buyer when the wholesaler assigns the buyer their rights to buy said property

**Balance Sheet:** A statement that shows a snapshot in time of the financial condition

**Balloon Payment:** A repayment of the outstanding principal sum made at the end of a loan period, interest only having been paid hitherto.

**Bandit Sign:** An actual sign used as a marketing tool used by real estate investors to find new property deals.

**Blue Collar:** Hourly paid workers that perform manual labor.

**Broker:** A real estate agent that once passes the broker's exam, is allowed to own a real estate firm and hire real estate agents to work for them.

**Built-in Equity:** Purchasing an asset that's less than its appraised value.

**Business Credit with a PG:** Unsecured business credit cards that you use for any purpose. These business credit card accounts do not show up on your personal credit reports, but the inquiries do. However, 100 Percent Financed can get these inquiries removed for you. The business credit accounts will show up on your personal credit reports if you default (do not make the minimum payment).

**Buy and Hold Strategy:** The investor closes on a cash flowing property and holds it so that the cash flow can support his or her lifestyle.

**Buyer's Agent:** A real estate agent whose sole responsibility is the best interest of the buyer with a formal contract.

**Cap Rate:** Ratio of Net Operating Income (NOI) to property asset value.

**Capital Gain:** A rise in the value of a capital asset (real property) that makes it worth more than the purchase price. Once the asset (real property) is sold, the difference in the purchase price and the sale price is taxed by governing officials.

**Caretaker:** The person who maintains the property for the owner providing services such as gardening, housekeeping and any day-to-day needs.

**Cash Closer:** Someone who purchases a property at full purchase price using all cash, meaning not a mortgage loan. A combination of savings, private loans, equity partner contributions, business loans, hard money loans.

**Cash Flow:** Gross revenue minus operating expenses, reserves and debt service. The profit that is left over is your cash flow.

**Cash-on-Cash Return:** The total cash received from a deal every year as a percentage of the total cash invested.

**Cash-Out Refinance:** A financial instrument that allows you to pull out the equity from an investment property. Most mortgage lenders will allow you to pull out 80% of the appraised value minus any debt owed on the property

**Closing:** The final step in executing a real estate transaction by transferring ownership of the property to the buyer. This is scheduled for a specific date.

**Closing Costs:** Costs that you have to bring to the closing table to pay for points, recording costs, title work, as well as other lender and attorney's fees.

**Clouded Title:** Any document, claim, unreleased lien or encumbrance that might invalidate or impair the title to real property. Clouded titles are normally discovered during a title search, and the seller must resolve them prior to closing.

**Code Enforcement:** A person in authority, usually an officer employed by the city or county who enforces laws, rules and regulations.

**Comps:** Properties with similar characteristics of a subject property whose value is being sought.

**Contingencies:** A condition or action that must be met for a real estate contract to become binding – (Appraisal, Financing, Title)

**Counter Offer:** Once a buyer submits an offer to purchase a property and the seller disagrees with the terms, the seller submits a counter offer which typically states that the seller will accept the buyers offer with a few changes being made.

**Deal Finder:** A listing/seller's agent, bird dog or wholesaler who finds investment properties for real estate investors.

**Deal Flow:** A consistent influx of investment properties via various sources, such as driving for dollars, MLS listings, real estate agents emailing investment opportunities, motivated sellers reaching out from bandit signs or direct mail campaigns, craiglist's postings, and wholesalers calling to present new investment properties.

**Debt-to-Credit Ratio:** Also referred to as debt utilization ratio. Your credit utilization ratio is a measure of how much you owe on your revolving credit (credit cards) relative to your maximum limit.

**Debt-to-Income Ratio:** The amount of debt you pay on a monthly basis compared to the overall income you receive on a monthly basis.

**Debt Service:** Debt you borrowed to acquire an asset. Examples are mortgages, private lenders, seller financing, hard money and business credit.

**Direct Mail:** Marketing material that can include brochures, postcards or sales letters that uses the United States Postal Service to deliver this printed material to your targeted audience, aka junk mail.

**Distressed House:** Any property that is under foreclosure or being sold, usually below market value, by the lender.

**Dual Agent:** A real estate agent who combines their role into one and works for both the buyer and the seller, aka transaction broker.

**Due Diligence:** Reasonable steps taken by a person in order to satisfy a legal requirement, especially in buying or selling something. Basically taking caution, performing calculations, reviewing documents, walking the property, etc.

**Duplex:** A house divided into two apartments with separate entrances.

**Entrepreneur:** A person who puts together and runs a business, taking on the financial risks associated with it.

**Equity:** Difference between what the asset is appraised at versus how much debt you owe on the asset. In some cases, you can pull out the equity using a cash-out refinance, and use the funds toward the down payment of your next deal.

**Exit Strategy:** An investor Knows what they eventually want to do with a property the day they purchase it. It's the method in which the investor intends to cash out of the property.

**FHA Mortgage:** FHA loan is a government backed mortgage insured by the Federal Housing Administration which protects the lender from loss if the borrower defaults on the loan.

**FICO Score:** This score ranges between 300 and 850. Higher scores indicate lower credit risk. Each individual has 65 credit scores for the FICO scoring model because each of the three national credit bureaus—Equifax, Experian and TransUnion—has its own database.

**Financial Instrument:** The legal documents that establish the rights and responsibilities of all parties involved in a transaction. There are two financing instrument (promissory note) and the security instrument (mortgage) in a real estate transaction.

**Flipping:** When a real estate investor buys a house, normally at a lower cost that needs repairs, and fixing it up and reselling it to make a profit.

**Forced Appreciation:** Managing the property with a focus on improving the profitability of it, such as increasing the revenue and decreasing the expenses.

**Full Rehab:** Can include replacing or repairing the roof, electrical components, plumbing, flooring, windows, kitchen, bathrooms and any other parts of the property.

**General Partners:** A person who joins with at least one other person to form a business or real estate partnership. A general partner has responsibility for the actions of the business. General partners can legally bind the business and is personally liable for all business debts and obligations. The general partner structures the deal.

**Gross Operating Income:** Gross revenue minus vacancy rate.

**Gross Revenue:** Total income you receive from an asset. Examples can be rental income, coined laundry, vending machines and application fees.

**HUD Settlement Statement:** A government document that itemizes all charges and credits to both the buyer and the seller for a real estate transaction.

**Hard Inquiries:** A potential lender reviews your credit because you applied for a line of credit.

**Hard Money:** A financial instrument where a private lender may lend you money to purchase and fix up a distressed asset. Most conventional lenders will not lend you money on an asset that is not livable. A hard money lender will, as long as the purchase price plus the rehab costs are less than 65% of the ARV. If you are not able to get the purchase price plus the rehab to be less than 65% of the ARV, you will have to bring the rest to closing.

**Hazard Insurance:** Structural coverage for a property such as fire damage, hail damage, theft, vandalism and more.

**Income Statement:** Also known as a profit & loss statement, is a report created by a company's management that shows the revenue, expenses, and loss for a given period.

**Installment Debt:** A financial instrument that is repaid by the borrower in regular installments. It repays in equal monthly payments, which include interest and a portion of the principal. It is a preferred method of consumer financing for big-ticket items such as cars, mortgages and appliances.

**Inspection Period:** The time frame during which a buyer has the opportunity to perform due diligence on a property they intend to buy.

**Institutional Buyer:** An institution that purchases properties in bulk for a discount, such as a mutual fund.

**Interest Only:** A payment structure that lets you delay the principal payment, but pay only the interest payment. The principal is normally due as a balloon payment.

**Interest Rate:** The percentage of the principal charged by the lender for the use of its money.

**Investor Loan:** Financing with specific terms for borrowers who intend to buy and sell or flip a property.

**Lease Option:** A type of contract used in both residential and commercial real estate in which a property owner and master tenant agree that, at the end of a specified rental period, the renter has the option to purchase the property. Lease options allow investors to obtain control over an asset without necessarily purchasing the asset.

**Letter of Intent:** A prospective buyer states an interest in a property while outlining the terms of the potential sale before committing to the purchase.

**Leverage:** The power to influence a person or situation in order to achieve a particular outcome.

**Limited Partners:** A partner in a company or venture who receives limited profits from the business and whose liability toward its debts is legally limited to the extent of his or her investment.

**Listing:** A property for sale that is advertised.

**Listing Agent:** A real estate agent who lists properties and works primarily with sellers. The listing agent should know the state of the property, as well as the motivation for the seller.

**Loan to Value:** A term used by lenders to express the ratio of a loan to the value of an asset purchased. The term is commonly used by banks and building societies to represent the ratio of the first mortgage line as a percentage of the total appraised value of real property.

**Master Lease Option:** The master lease gives control of the property to include managing, operations, and the right to rent out the property. The option portion offers the opportunity to purchase the property during a certain amount of time for a certain price.

**Maximum Allowable Offer:** A formula for you to use when purchasing a distressed asset using hard money. (.65 ARV–Repairs) = MAO. If you are wholesaling a distressed asset, use the formula: MAO = (.65 ARV–Repairs–wholesale fee).

**Mortgage Banker:** Someone who works for a specific bank and can only offer mortgage products that this particular bank has to offer.

**Mortgage Broker:** This person brokers mortgages. He or she has relationships with many mortgage bankers and can find the best mortgage lender for you.

**Mortgage Lender:** Any person who provides mortgages.

**Motivated Seller:** The owner of a property is eager to sell fast due to economic hardships or a number of other personal reasons.

**Multi-family:** Five or more rental units under one roof.

**Multiple listing Service (MLS):** A marketing database for real estate agents that provides information about properties for sale.

**Multi-unit:** More than one rental unit sold under one realtor in a purchased portfolio.

**Natural Market Appreciation:** When the demand for rental properties outweighs the supply available.

**Net Operating Income (NOI):** Gross operating income minus operating expenses. This equation does not include debt service. The NOI is used to calculate the asset's value.

**Neighborhood Ranks:** Neighborhoods normally rank from A to D. (A) neighborhoods are broken down from a 4 to 5.9 % cap rates, (B) neighborhoods rank from 6 to 7.9%, (C) neighborhoods rank from 8 to 10%, and (D) neighborhoods rank from 10 to 12%. (A) areas have the highest appreciation, minimum risks, newer properties in affluent neighborhoods and minimum returns. (D) areas have the opposite of (A) areas by having the lowest appreciation, highest risks, older buildings, maximum returns, and less desirable neighborhoods. (B) and (C) areas fall somewhere in between. The class you want to invest in, based on risk tolerance, amount of funds available, and type of returns wanting to receive must be determined.

**No Money Down:** Not having to bring any funds to the closing table. No money down can happen if you purchase a distressed asset using hard money. Regarding multifamily, you as the syndicator may not have to put any money down, but your partners may.

**Operating Expenses:** Expenses incurred to operate an asset. This does not include debt service. Examples are taxes, insurance, property management fees, utilities and lawn care services.

**Out-of-Pocket Money:** Money the buyer uses for expenses outside of the mortgage during the sales process to include, but not limited to, home inspection, appraisal fees, closing costs, attorney fees and loan origination fees.

**Passive Income:** A stream of income earned with little effort by the recipient to maintain it.

**Penalties:** A punishment imposed for breaking the rules associated with a contract.

**Pocket Listing:** The property for sale is never advertised and the broker holds a signed listing agreement with the seller giving the broker exclusive rights to sell such property.

**Points:** A point is 1% of the total amount of money you are borrowing. So, if you are charged three points on a $100,000 loan, you have to repay $103,000 at maturity of the loan.

**Portfolio Package:** Buying several properties in a single transaction.

**Price Points:** The maximum price a seller is willing to accept for their property, and the maximum price a buyer is willing to pay for a property.

**Principal:** The total loan amount due to satisfy the payoff amount of the underlying obligation, less interest or other charges.

**Private Money:** A friend, family member, or colleague (not institutional) who gives you money to invest. Private money can come in the form of an investor or a lender. A private investor partners with you and has equity. However, the private investor is paid based on the profitability of the asset. A private lender only lends money for interest and/or points. A private lender's profit is not based upon the profitability of the asset.

**Prepayment:** The settlement of a loan before its official due date.

**Pre-qualified:** When a lender performs a review of a person's financial situation in order to tell how much of a loan they can get.

**Pro forma:** The method of calculating a property's cash flow projections.

**Profit & Loss Statement:** A financial statement that depicts a business' operating performance to show revenue, expenses and net income.

**Promissory Note:** A signed document containing a written promise to pay a stated sum to a specified person or the bearer at a specified date or on demand.

**Property Inspection:** A third party does an inspection on a property for any outstanding problems that may affect the value and the safety of the property.

**Property Management:** Overseeing and managing the day to day operations of a property that is owned by another individual or entity.

**Purchase & Option Agreement:** An investor taking control of a property with an option to purchase it at a later date.

**Purchase & Sales Agreement:** A contract between the buyer and seller to acquire a property, aka sales contract and agreement of sale.

**Quadplex:** A small residential building with four apartments, aka fourplex.

**Qualified Buyer:** A person who is seeking property to purchase and has the financial ability to complete the purchase.

**Real Estate Owned (REO):** Property owned by a lender after an unsuccessful sale at a foreclosure auction.

**Realtor:** A person who acts as an agent for the sale and purchase of buildings and land, aka real estate agent.

**Refinance:** When a borrower gets a new mortgage to replace the existing mortgage with better interest term and rate.

**Renovation:** Restoring something such as property to its former state.

**Reserves:** A set amount of cash determined by a lender that the borrower must keep on hand after paying the down payment on a property for a set amount of time to qualify for a mortgage.

**Residential Mortgage:** A loan in which the property functions as collateral.

**Revolving Debt:** A financial instrument with a limit on how much you can borrow. The amount you use within that limit is up to you. Most revolving loans can be credit cards or lines of credit, where the borrower makes charges, pays them off, and continues to make charges.

**Section 8:** Housing and Urban Development (HUD) assists low-income people with rental payments on their behalf to private landlords.

**Seller Financing:** The person selling the property lends the buyer a portion or all of the money for the purchase. The buyer and seller execute a promissory note or a junior (secondary) mortgage, providing an interest rate, repayment schedule and consequences of default. In commercial mortgages, most mortgage lenders will allow the seller to hold a 10% note and no more.

**Single-family:** Four or less rental units under one roof.

**Soft Costs:** Costs incurred on an asset before you purchase it, such as property inspection fees, traveling expenses, appraisals and attorney's fees to form an entity.

**Syndication:** An effective way for investors to pool their financial and intellectual resources to invest in properties and projects much bigger than they could afford or manage on their own.

**Tenant:** A person who occupies land or property rented from a landlord.

**Trailing 12:** A term for various data of the past twelve months.

**Transactional Broker:** Third-party real estate services provided to buyers and sellers without being legally responsible to the buyer or seller. These services can include: helping the buyer draft the purchase offer; help the seller decide on an asking price and much more.

**Total Out-of-Pocket Expenses:** Soft costs, closing costs and down payment money that comes out of your pockets and your partner's pockets.

**Underwriter:** A real estate underwriter takes into consideration the loan on a property and the borrowers financial position to determine risks associated with the lender.

**Upfront Fees:** Money paid upfront such as the down payment, home appraisal and closing costs.

**Vacancy Rate:** A percentage of the gross revenue you won't receive since not all tenants pay rent. The vacancy rate is normally set at 5% of the gross revenue.

**Value:** Ratio of NOI to cap rate.

**Wholesaling:** The investor gets a property under contract and assigns his contract to an end buyer for a fee.

**Yearly Cash Flow:** The money moving in and out of a business over a period of a year.

**Yield Play:** An investor acquiring an investment property that's fully occupied producing cash flow with little to no repairs needed at the time of purchase.

# Index

## 100

100% occupied .................................. 99, 120, 122, 142, 149
100percentfinanced.com ...... v, xi, 21, 31, 48–50, 84, 122, 127, 136, 139, 149, 211, 212, 214, 215
100PF .................................. 7, 31, 32, 39, 126, 136, 206, 215

## A

acquisition fee ............................................... 101, 227
affirmations ...................................... 61, 64, 207–210, 212
After Repair Value ........................................... 75, 227
  ARV .................. 75, 77–79, 170–172, 177, 181, 182, 227, 235, 237
amortized ............................................... 79, 120, 140
analysis ...................................... 77, 84, 99, 106, 178, 205
analyze .................................. 40, 63, 64, 135, 136, 139, 197
appraisal ............. 77, 79, 80, 93, 124, 140, 146, 172, 227, 230, 239, 243
appraisal contingency ........................................... 140
appraisals ........................................... 83, 90, 121, 243
appreciation .......................... 51, 90, 93, 94, 96–98, 227, 238
assets .......................................... 16, 37, 42, 91, 99, 199
assign ...................................... 131, 153, 171, 192, 196, 199
attorneys .................................. 61, 62, 83, 105, 186, 187, 206

# B

balance sheet . . . . . . . . . . . . . . . . . . . . . . . . . . . . . . . . . . . . . . . . . . . . 205, 228
balance transfer . . . . . . . . . . . . . . . . . . . . . . . . . . . . . . . . . . . . . . . . . . 125, 126
balance transfer checks . . . . . . . . . . . . . . . . . . . . . . . . . . . . . . . . . . . . 125, 126
balloon payment . . . . . . . . . . . . . . . . . . . . . . . . . . . . . . . . . 90, 91, 120, 228, 235
bandit signs . . . . . . . . . . . . . . . . . . . . . . . . . . . . . . . . . . . . . 167, 169, 193, 231
bankruptcies . . . . . . . . . . . . . . . . . . . . . . . . . . . . . . . . . . . . . . . . . . . . . . 48–50
Beachbody on Demand . . . . . . . . . . . . . . . . . . . . . . . . . . . . . . . . . . . . . . . . . 60
billboards . . . . . . . . . . . . . . . . . . . . . . . . . . . . . . . . . . . . 32, 33, 39, 40, 54, 131
binding agreement . . . . . . . . . . . . . . . . . . . . . . . . . . . . . . . . . . . . . . . . . . . 184
blue collar . . . . . . . . . . . . . . . . . . . . . . . . . . . . . . . . . . . . . . . . . . . . . . 109, 228
broker . . . . 7, 101, 117–119, 123, 132, 142, 147, 197, 205, 228, 232, 237, 239, 243
building permit . . . . . . . . . . . . . . . . . . . . . . . . . . . . . . . . . . . . . . . . . . . . . . 81
built-in equity . . . . . . . . . . . . . . . . . . . . . . . . . . . . . . . . 93, 96, 98, 111, 140, 228
business credit . . . . . . . . . 16, 17, 39, 45, 47, 48, 50, 74, 76–79, 84, 122, 124–127, 152, 156, 203–205, 215, 228, 231

# C

cash . . . . . . . . . . 12, 13, 17, 18, 26–28, 31, 39, 41–43, 51–53, 70, 73–84, 88–99, 101–103, 105, 106, 110, 111, 120, 122, 124–126, 129, 132, 136, 139, 148, 151, 152, 155, 157, 166, 171, 182, 192, 193, 195–197, 200, 203–205, 207, 217–221
cash advances . . . . . . . . . . . . . . . . . . . . . . . . . . . . . . . . . . . . . . . . . . . . 51, 126
cash closers . . . . . . . . . . . . . . . . . . . . . . . . . . . . . . . . . . . . . . . . . . . . . . . . 195
cash flow . . 12, 26–28, 31, 41, 42, 70, 73, 74, 76–82, 84, 88, 89, 90, 91, 92, 94, 95, 97–99, 101, 102, 106, 136, 139, 148, 171, 203, 205, 207, 229, 240, 244
cash flowing . . . . . . . . . . . . . . . . 12, 39, 41, 42, 52, 70, 81, 82, 84, 90, 155, 229
cash-on-cash return . . . . . . . . . . . . 91, 92, 110, 111, 122, 136, 139, 204, 205, 229
cash-out refinance . . . . . . . . . . . . . . . . . . . . . . . . . . . 93, 94, 96, 97, 98, 230, 232
charge-offs . . . . . . . . . . . . . . . . . . . . . . . . . . . . . . . . . . . . . . . . . . . . . . . . . . 49
city inspector . . . . . . . . . . . . . . . . . . . . . . . . . . . . . . . . . . . . . . . . . . . . . . . . 81
city ordinances . . . . . . . . . . . . . . . . . . . . . . . . . . . . . . . . . . . . . . . . . . . . . . 167
closed accounts . . . . . . . . . . . . . . . . . . . . . . . . . . . . . . . . . . . . . . . . . . . . . . 49
closing . . . . . 17, 31, 61, 69, 74, 75, 77, 79–82, 84, 85, 89, 90, 93, 94, 96, 97, 99, 119–122, 139–142, 145–149, 151, 154, 157, 184, 186–188, 191, 192, 196, 199, 220, 227, 230, 235, 239, 243

closing costs . . . . . . . . . 17, 75, 77–80, 83, 90, 93, 94, 96, 97, 119, 121, 146, 154, 227, 230, 239, 243

closing table . . . . . . . . . . . . . . . . . . . . . . . . . . . . . . . 122, 123, 147, 199, 230, 239
clouded title . . . . . . . . . . . . . . . . . . . . . . . . . . . . . . . . . . . . . . . . . . . . 191, 230
code enforcement . . . . . . . . . . . . . . . . . . . . . . . . . . . . . . . . . . . 167, 169, 230
collection accounts . . . . . . . . . . . . . . . . . . . . . . . . . . . . . . . . . . . . . . . . 49, 50
commercial mortgages . . . . . . . . . . . . . . . . . . . . . . . . . . . . . . . . . . . . 81, 242
commercial real estate agents . . . . . . . . . . . . . . . . . . . . . . . . . . . . . . . . . 133
commission . . . . . . . . . . . . . . . . . . . . . . . . . . . . . . . . . . . . . . . . . 52, 132, 227
commitment letter . . . . . . . . . . . . . . . . . . . . . . . . . . . . . . . . . . . . . . . . . . 146
comparable sales . . . . . . . . . . . . . . . . . . . . . . . . . . . . . . . . . . . . . . . . . . . . 78
comps . . . . . . . . . . . . . . . . . . . . . . . . . . . . . . . . . . . . . . . . . 172, 177, 181, 230
contingencies . . . . . . . . . . . . . . . . . . . . . . . . . . . . . . . . . . . . . . . . 140, 148, 230
contract . . . . . . 52, 93, 103, 106, 107, 131, 134, 140, 141, 143, 144, 153, 154, 170, 171, 180, 184–186, 188, 191, 192, 194–196, 199, 229, 230, 236, 239, 241, 244

contractors . . . . . . . . . . . . . . . . . . . . . . 62, 81, 123, 128, 145, 179, 209, 218
convenience checks . . . . . . . . . . . . . . . . . . . . . . . . . . . . . . . . . . . . . . 125, 126
conventional investment mortgage . . . . . . . . . . . . . . . . . . . . . . . . . . . . . . 77
conventional lender . . . . . . . . . . . . . . . . . . . . . . . . . . . . . . . . . . . . . . . . . 196
corrugated plastic sheets . . . . . . . . . . . . . . . . . . . . . . . . . . . . . . . . . . . . . 168
counter offer . . . . . . . . . . . . . . . . . . . . . . . . . . . . . . . . . . . . . . . . . . . . . . . 231
county records . . . . . . . . . . . . . . . . . . . . . . . . . . . . . . . . . . . . . . . . . . . . . 187
credit . . . . . . . . . . . . 4, 15–17, 19, 23, 26, 27, 39–41, 43, 45–51, 53, 54, 68, 74, 76, 78, 79, 82–84, 98, 117, 118, 122–128, 130, 132, 134, 145, 147, 148, 151, 152, 154–156, 200, 201, 203–205, 207, 208, 210, 215, 228, 231, 233, 234, 242

credit cards . . . . . . . . . . . . . . . . . . . . 19, 23, 46, 50, 51, 123–127, 228, 231, 242
credit line increases . . . . . . . . . . . . . . . . . . . . . . . . . . . . . . . . . . 16, 50, 51, 127
credit repair . . . . . . . . . . . . . . . . . . . . . . . . . . . . . . . 48–50, 116, 124, 128, 148, 156
credit report . . . . . . . . . . . . . . . . . 15, 47, 49, 51, 53, 54, 117, 118, 124, 127, 130, 134

# D

deal . . . . . . . xi, 17, 18, 28, 31, 39–41, 50, 52, 55, 68–70, 73, 74, 77, 79, 80, 84, 87–93, 98, 100, 101, 103, 105–107, 112, 114, 117, 120–123, 131–135, 139–142, 144–146, 148, 149, 152, 154–156, 159, 170, 177, 181, 183–186, 192, 195, 196, 199–201, 203–205, 229, 231, 232, 234

debt . . . . . 12, 15, 16, 20, 31, 50, 68, 79, 84, 88, 96, 99, 106, 110, 123, 156, 171, 204, 205, 229, 230–232, 238, 239

*Index*: B–D

debt service ...... 12, 31, 79, 84, 88, 96, 99, 110, 171, 204, 229, 231, 238, 239
debt-to-credit ..................... 15, 19, 23, 41, 46, 51, 124, 130, 151, 231
debt-to-income ............................. 15, 19, 23, 51, 118, 124, 231
debt-to-Income ratio ............................. 19, 23, 51, 118, 124, 231
direct mail ...................... 159, 160, 162, 163, 167, 201, 217, 231, 232
direct mail marketing campaign ...................................... 167
distressed asset ..................................... 74, 234, 237, 239
distressed house ............................................. 75, 232
down payment ..... 17, 43, 47, 48, 76, 77–81, 84, 89, 90, 93, 95, 98, 102, 105, 121, 128, 151, 153–155, 232, 242, 243
driving for dollars ........................................... 159, 231
dual agent ................................................. 132, 232
due diligence ............... 94, 140, 142–145, 149, 170, 178, 180, 232, 235
duplex ........................... 51, 85, 88, 90, 93, 112, 135, 205, 232

# E

earnest money .............................................. 140–142
an employee .............................................. 55, 56, 162
entrepreneur(s) ........ vii, 5, 21, 56, 63, 66, 71–73, 85–87, 100, 114, 115, 126, 127, 137, 146, 192, 203, 206, 208, 210, 212, 232
equity ........ 17, 78, 79, 92, 93, 95–98, 100, 111, 121, 122, 140, 162, 171, 205, 228–230, 232, 240
evictions ................................................. 49, 50, 103
exit strategy ........................................... 97, 98, 120, 233

# F

fair price .................................................... 106
FHA mortgage
 FHA .................................................... 51, 84, 233
FICO score ...................... 15, 19, 23, 39, 45–48, 50, 83, 118, 233
finance ........... 72, 73, 77, 78, 80, 81, 89, 91, 95, 100, 122–124, 156, 195
financial documents ............................................. 134
 PFS ................................................. 117, 134, 136
financial freedom .......... 1, 6, 7, 9, 13, 14, 17, 25, 26, 28, 31, 39, 45, 51, 53, 60, 66, 67, 69, 88, 135, 151, 200, 203, 205, 211

financial instrument . . . . . . . . . . . . . . . . . . . . . . 28, 40, 80, 230, 233–235, 242
financially free . . . . . . . . . . . . . . . . . . . . . . . 7, 14, 21, 28, 31, 61, 65, 73, 209, 210
flipping . . . . . . . . . . . . . . . . . . . . . . . . . . . . . . . . . . . . . . . . . . . 13, 78, 204, 233
forced appreciation . . . . . . . . . . . . . . . . . . . . . . . . . . . . . . . . . . . . . . . 227, 233
foreclosures . . . . . . . . . . . . . . . . . . . . . . . . . . . . . . . . . . . . . . . . . . . 48, 49, 87
foreign file . . . . . . . . . . . . . . . . . . . . . . . . . . . . . . . . . . . . . . . . . . . . . . . . . 127
free consultation . . . . . . . . . . . . . . . . . . . . . . . . . . . . . . . . . . . . . . . 48, 122, 127
full rehab . . . . . . . . . . . . . . . . . . . . . . . . . . . . . . . . . . . . . . . . . . . . . 74, 82, 234
funding . . . . . . . . . . . . . . . . . . . . . . . . . . . . . . . . . . . . . . . 45–48, 126, 127, 220

# G

general contractor . . . . . . . . . . . . . . . . . . . . . . . . . . . . . . . . . . . . . . . . . 81, 99
general partners . . . . . . . . . . . . . . . . . . . . . . . . . . . . . . . . . . . . . . . . . . . . 234
Gmail . . . . . . . . . . . . . . . . . . . . . . . . . . . . . . . . . . . . . . . . 62, 163–165, 218, 221
Google voice . . . . . . . . . . . . . . . . . . . . . . . . . . . . . . . . . . . . . 62, 164, 165, 193
gross operating income . . . . . . . . . . . . . . . . . . . . . . . . . . . . . . . . . . . 234, 238

# H

hammer stapler . . . . . . . . . . . . . . . . . . . . . . . . . . . . . . . . . . . . . . . . . . . . . 169
hard inquiry . . . . . . . . . . . . . . . . . . . . . . . . . . . . . . . . . . . . . . . . . . . . . . 50, 118
hard money . . . . . . . . . . . . . . . . . . . 74–82, 99, 131, 195, 229, 231, 234, 237, 239
Hard Moneylender . . . . . . . . . . . . . . . . . . . . . . . . . . . . . . . . . . . . . . . . 74, 195
  HML . . . . . . . . . . . . . . . . . . . . . . . . . . . . . . . . . . . . . . . . . . . . . 75, 76, 78, 80
hard pull . . . . . . . . . . . . . . . . . . . . . . . . . . . . . . . . . . . . . . . . . . . . . . . . . . . . 50
hazard insurance . . . . . . . . . . . . . . . . . . . . . . . . . . . . . . . . . . . . . . . 89, 95, 235
holding costs . . . . . . . . . . . . . . . . . . . . . . . . . . . . . . . . . . . . . . . . 76, 78, 80, 82
HUD . . . . . . . . . . . . . . . . . . . . . . . . . . . . . . . . . . . . . . . . . . . 146, 199, 234, 242
HUD-1 Settlement Statement . . . . . . . . . . . . . . . . . . . . . . . . . . . . . . . . . . . 146

# I

income statement . . . . . . . . . . . . . . . . . . . . . . . . . . . . . . . . . . . . . . . . 205, 235
income-producing asset . . . . . . . . . . . . . . . . . . . . . . . . . . . . . . . . . 28, 73, 107
inquiries . . . . . . . . . . . . . . . . . . . . . . . . . . . . . 15, 19, 23, 46, 48, 50, 228, 234

Index: D–I

inspection period ................................... 153, 154, 185, 235
installment debt ......................................... 20, 124, 235
institutional buyer ...................................... 197, 198, 235
insurance broker ............................................... 142
interest only ........................................... 89, 228, 235
interest rate ................. 51, 76, 77, 78, 90, 100, 119, 120, 140, 236, 242
interest-only ........................................... 76, 78, 90, 95
investment .......... 12–14, 27, 39, 45, 51, 74, 77, 79–81, 84, 87, 90, 92, 99, 100, 107, 113, 133, 143, 153, 160, 172, 230, 231, 236, 244
investment mortgage ..................................... 77, 90, 100
investment property ........................ 13, 39, 45, 51, 172, 230, 244
investor loan ..................................... 79, 89, 91, 94–98, 236

# J

judgments .............................................. 48–50, 140

# L

late payments ............................................... 48, 49
lease .............................. 11, 20, 42, 43, 100–103, 105, 171, 237
lease option ........................... 13, 100–103, 105, 171, 236, 237
lenders ............ 16, 46, 47, 76, 83, 84, 93, 94, 118, 120, 121, 124, 152, 195, 200, 206, 209, 230, 231, 234, 237, 242
letter of intent ......................................... 136, 139, 236
leverage ............................................. 16, 81, 92, 236
listing ......... 79, 83, 88, 103–105, 117–119, 129, 131–133, 135, 142, 143, 145, 219, 231, 236, 238, 239
listing agent ....................... 103–105, 118, 119, 132, 133, 145, 236
loan ........ 20, 47, 50, 76–79, 82, 84, 89, 91, 93–98, 100, 122, 147, 195, 196, 228, 229, 233, 236, 237, 239, 240, 242, 243
local tax office ................................................ 142
loopnet.com ................................................. 133

# M

Marcus and Millichap . . . . . . . . . . . . . . . . . . . . . . . . . . . . . . . . . . . . . . . . . . 114
market . . . . . . . . . . 7, 14, 18, 27, 28, 40, 42, 63, 80, 81, 84, 93, 96–99, 109–115, 117, 131, 136, 154, 158, 184, 188, 192, 194, 201, 219, 232, 238
market data . . . . . . . . . . . . . . . . . . . . . . . . . . . . . . . . . . . . . . . . . . . . . . . . . 63
marketing costs . . . . . . . . . . . . . . . . . . . . . . . . . . . . . . . . . . . . . . . . . . . . 153
Master Lease Option . . . . . . . . . . . . . . . . . . . . . . . . . . . . . . . . . . 100–103, 237
MLO . . . . . . . . . . . . . . . . . . . . . . . . . . . . . . . . . . . . . . . . . . . . . . . . . 103–105
Maximum Allowable Offer . . . . . . . . . . . . . . . . . . . . . . . . . . . . . . 170, 181, 237
MAO . . . . . . . . . . . . . . . . . . . . . . . . . . . . . . . . . . . . . . . . 170, 181, 182, 184, 237
medical bills . . . . . . . . . . . . . . . . . . . . . . . . . . . . . . . . . . . . . . . . . . . . . 49, 50
mindset . . . . . . . . . . . . . . . . . . . . . . . . . . . . . 40, 42, 56, 114, 131, 156, 200, 212
model . . . . . . . . . . . . . . . . . 74, 81, 84, 87, 99, 107, 113, 117, 131, 134, 171, 177, 233
monthly living expenses . . . . . . . . . . . . . . . . . . . . . . . . . . . . . . . 18, 19, 22, 23, 25
monthly mortgage (PITI) . . . . . . . . . . . . . . . . . . . . . . . . . . . . . . . . . . . . . . . 20
mortgage . . . . . . . . . . 7, 16, 17, 19, 20, 50, 51, 63, 76–78, 83, 84, 89, 90, 93–96, 98, 100, 101, 103, 104, 117–124, 128, 129, 132, 134, 141, 142, 145, 146, 171, 191, 205, 206, 209, 229, 230, 233, 237, 239, 242
mortgage banker . . . . . . . . . . . . . . . . . . . . . . . . . . . . . . . . . . . . . . . . . . . 237
mortgage broker(s) . . . . . . . . . . . . . . . 7, 63, 101, 117, 119, 123, 128, 129, 205, 237
mortgage lender . . . . . . . . . . . . . . . . . . . . . . . . . 78, 100, 103, 134, 142, 145, 237
motivated seller . . . . . . . . . . 156, 157, 170, 171, 178, 180, 184, 217, 221, 222, 237
multi-family . . . . . . . . . . . . . . . . . . . . . . . . . . . . . . . . . . . . . . . . . 109, 121, 238
multi-unit . . . . . . . . . . . . . . . 27, 48, 74, 81, 84, 109, 112, 120, 139, 149, 215, 238
Multi-unit Acquisition Program . . . . . . . . . . . . . . . . . . . . . . . . . . . . . . . . . . . 84
MAP . . . . . . . . . . . . . . . . . . . . . . . . . . . . . . . . . . . . . . . . . 84, 91, 121, 136, 144
multi-unit property . . . . . . . . . . . . . . . . . . . . . . . . . . . . . . . . . . . . . . . . 27, 139
Multiple Listing Service . . . . . . . . . . . . . . . . . . . . . . . . . . . . . . . . . 83, 133, 238
MLS . . . . . . . . . . . . . . . . . . . . . . . . . . . . . . . . . . . . . . . . . . . . . 83, 197, 231, 238

# N

natural market appreciation . . . . . . . . . . . . . . . . . . . . . . . . . . . . . . . 93, 96, 238
neighborhood A . . . . . . . . . . . . . . . . . . . . . . . . . . . . . . . . . . . . . . . . . . . . 110
neighborhood D . . . . . . . . . . . . . . . . . . . . . . . . . . . . . . . . . . . . . . . . . . . . 110
neighborhood ranks . . . . . . . . . . . . . . . . . . . . . . . . . . . . . . . . . . . . . . . . . 238

*Index: I–N*

Net Operating Income .................................... 110, 229, 238
NOI .......................................... 110, 111, 229, 238, 244
net worth ................................. 16, 17, 19, 23, 40, 54, 128
network .... 6, 54, 83, 86, 100, 107, 115, 151, 152, 154–156, 186, 196, 198, 203
networking ...... 4, 6, 17, 54, 59, 64, 65, 69, 70, 79, 83, 86, 112–114, 131, 133, 148, 153, 193, 198, 201
networking events ..................... 54, 64, 86, 113, 114, 131, 133, 198

## O

occupancy .............................................. 74, 103, 104
occupancy rates ............................................... 104
operating expenses ............. 12, 88, 90, 96, 110, 141, 147, 229, 238, 239
option to purchase ....................................... 102, 236, 241
out-of-pocket cash ........................................... 17, 18, 91
out-of-pocket costs .................... 80, 91, 101, 120–124, 129, 132, 154
out-of-pocket money .................................. 83, 84, 119, 239

## P

P90X3 ...................................................... 60
partner ............. 18, 39, 58, 59, 76, 80, 100, 101, 118–120, 122, 152, 154, 203, 218, 229, 234, 236, 243
partnership(s) ......................................... 17, 81, 100, 234
passive income .......... 1, 12, 21, 25, 27, 28, 31, 67, 70, 81, 88, 89, 155, 156, 201, 205, 208, 239
Passive Income > Living Expenses ..................................... 25
PILE ................................................. 25, 29, 67
paydex score ................................................. 47
permits ................................................ 20, 81, 152
personal financial statement ............................ 21, 42, 136, 203
personal guarantee ............................................. 47
points ................. 13, 76–78, 90, 91, 100, 114, 119, 172, 230, 239, 240
portfolio..... 5, 7, 25–28, 42, 69, 70, 82, 112, 113, 115, 121, 203, 206, 238, 240
portfolio package ............................................. 240
pre-qualification letter ................................. 118, 119, 134
pre-qualified .......................................... 77, 119, 240

prepayment . . . . . . . . . . . . . . . . . . . . . . . . . . . . . . . . . . . . . . . . . . . 76–78, 240
prepayment penalties . . . . . . . . . . . . . . . . . . . . . . . . . . . . . . . . . . . . . 76–78
principal . . . . . . . . . . . . . . . . . . . . . . . . . . . . . 76, 89, 95, 228, 235, 236, 240
private lender . . . . . . . . . . . . . . . . . . . . . . . . . . . . . . . 76, 90, 122, 234, 240
private money . . . . . . . . . . . . . . . . . . . . . . . . . . . . . . . . . . . . . . . . . . . . . 240
pro forma . . . . . . . . . . . . . . . . . . . . . . . . . . . . . . . . . . . . . . . . . . . . . . 90, 240
Profit & Loss statement(s) . . . . . . . . . . . . . . . . . . . . . . . . . . . 47, 141, 235, 240
  P & Ls . . . . . . . . . . . . . . . . . . . . . . . . . . . . . . . . . . . . . . . . . . . . . . . . . . 47
promissory note . . . . . . . . . . . . . . . . . . . . . . . . . . . . . . . . . . 100, 233, 241, 242
properties . . . . . 52, 64, 68, 74, 82, 87, 99, 109, 111, 112, 115, 127, 133, 139, 142, 153, 155, 156, 159, 160, 162, 166, 172–174, 177, 178, 182, 184, 188, 192, 194, 196–198, 200, 203, 204, 206, 221, 230, 231, 235, 236, 238, 240, 243
property inspection(s) . . . . . . . . . . . . . . 83, 90, 105, 121, 144, 145, 203, 241, 243
property management . . . . . . . . . . . . . . . . . . . . 7, 52, 102, 124, 143, 147, 239, 241
property manager . . . . . . . . . . . . . . . . . . . . . . . . . . . . . . . . 52, 68, 103, 105, 144
property taxes . . . . . . . . . . . . . . . . . . . . . . . . . . . . . . . . . . . . . . . . . 89, 95, 225
*Proverbs* . . . . . . . . . . . . . . . . . . . . . . . . . . . . . . . . . . . . . . . . 56, 57, 58, 71, 85
purchase and sale agreement . . . . . . . . . . . . . . . . . . . . . . . 120, 184, 185, 191, 241
purchase option agreement . . . . . . . . . . . . . . . . . . . . . . . . . . . . . . . 184, 185, 241
purchase price . . . . . . 18, 77–79, 101, 105, 119–121, 132, 133, 135, 140, 143, 146, 153, 229, 234, 235

# Q

quadplex . . . . . . . . . . . . . . . . . . . . . . . . . . . . . . . . . . . . . . . . . . . . 69, 83, 86, 241
qualified buyer . . . . . . . . . . . . . . . . . . . . . . . . . . . . . . . . . . . . . . . . . . . . 192, 241

# R

real estate agent . . . . . . . . . . 7, 88, 121, 141, 142, 220, 228, 229, 232, 236, 241
real estate groups . . . . . . . . . . . . . . . . . . . . . . . . . . . . . . . . . . . . . . . . . . 64, 114
real estate industry . . . . . . . . . . . . . . . . . . . . . . . . . . . . . . . . . . . . . . . . . . . 7, 62
real estate investing . . . . . . . . 4, 5, 13, 16, 17, 21, 51, 52, 54, 58, 59, 62, 63, 65, 69, 72, 73, 80, 82, 83, 86, 99, 101, 106, 113, 114, 118, 122, 128, 130, 131, 134, 136, 137, 156, 158, 208, 210
Real Estate Investor Association or Real Estate Investor Alliance . . . . . . . . . 114
  REIA . . . . . . . . . . . . . . . . . . . . . . . . . . . . . . . . . . . . . . . . . . . . . 114, 193, 198

*Index:* N–R

Real Estate Owned ............................................. 75, 241
REO ...................................................... 75, 77, 241
realtor(s) .......... 61, 62, 90, 159, 178, 185, 187, 193, 197, 198, 220, 238, 241
refinance ....... 51, 76–78, 80, 93, 94, 96–98, 123, 124, 205, 230, 232, 242
rehabilitator(s) ............................................. 153, 156, 172
reinvest ...................................................... 43, 98, 204
renovation ................................................... 74, 172, 242
rent proration ................................................... 122, 147
rent roll ............................................................. 141
rental unit(s) .................. 7, 26, 27, 41, 42, 67, 69, 70, 82, 147, 238, 243
repair allowance(s) ....................................... 123, 145, 147
repossessions ........................................................ 49
reserves ....................... 12, 83, 84, 88, 90, 110, 121, 152, 229, 242
residential mortgage ........................................... 84, 242
resignation letter ................... 4, 25, 33, 37, 51, 82, 204, 209, 210, 212
retirement ..................................... 17, 76, 120, 122, 134, 195
retirement accounts ............................... 17, 120, 122, 134, 195
revenue ....................... 88, 94, 110, 204, 229, 233–235, 240, 244
revolving debt ............................................... 20, 124, 242
rule ............................................................ 135, 139

# S

savings ........................... 11, 17, 23, 26, 41, 76, 91, 122, 195, 229
seasoned businesses ............................................... 48
Section 8 ............................................. 94, 103, 110, 242
security deposits ........................................... 122, 123, 147
seller financing ...................... 18, 74, 105, 120, 132, 140, 231, 242
sellers script ...................................................... 171
single-family ............... 27, 28, 74, 76, 79, 81, 85, 99, 102, 131, 154, 243
soft costs ..................................... 17, 83, 90, 121, 154, 243
square footage ............................................ 172, 179, 223
sublease ..................................................... 11, 42
syndication ...................................................... 243

## T

tax assessor . . . . . . . . . . . . . . . . . . . . . . . . . . . . . . . . . . . . . . . . . . . . . 159–161, 181
tax liens . . . . . . . . . . . . . . . . . . . . . . . . . . . . . . . . . . . . . . . . . . . . . . . . . . . 49, 50
tax records . . . . . . . . . . . . . . . . . . . . . . . . . . . . . . . . . . . . . . . . . . . . . . 162, 197
tenant . . . . . . . . . . . . . . . . . . . . . . . . . . . . . . . . . 11, 52, 78, 94, 123, 236, 243
title . . . . . . . . . . . . . . . . . . 90, 121, 140, 145, 166, 171, 181, 186–188, 191, 192, 230
title company . . . . . . . . . . . . . . . . . . . . . . . . . . . . . . . . . . 171, 186–188, 191, 192
title contingency . . . . . . . . . . . . . . . . . . . . . . . . . . . . . . . . . . . . . . . . . . . . . . . 140
total out-of-pocket expenses . . . . . . . . . . . . . . . . . . . . . . . . . . . . . . . . . . . 82, 243
trailing . . . . . . . . . . . . . . . . . . . . . . . . . . . . . . . . . . . . . . . . . . . . . . . . . 12 141, 243
transactional broker . . . . . . . . . . . . . . . . . . . . . . . . . . . . . . . . . . . . . . . . . 132, 243

## U

underwriter(s) . . . . . . . . . . . . . . . . . . . . . . . . . . . . . . . . . . . . . . . . . . . . . . . 81, 243
unit goal . . . . . . . . . . . . . . . . . . . . . . . . . . . . . . . . . . . . . . . . . . . . . . . . 26, 28, 29
units . . . . . 7, 18, 25–29, 31, 41, 42, 52, 67, 69, 70, 81, 82, 84, 100, 111, 144, 147, 203, 206, 238, 243
upfront fees . . . . . . . . . . . . . . . . . . . . . . . . . . . . . . . . . . . . . . . . . . . 48, 76, 77, 243

## V

vacancy rate . . . . . . . . . . . . . . . . . . . . . . . . . . . . . . . . . . . . . . . . . . 88, 95, 234, 244
value . . . . . . . . . . . vii, 3, 16, 74, 75, 77, 78, 88, 92, 93, 95–97, 99–101, 110, 111, 139–141, 146, 172, 183, 219, 227–230, 232, 237, 238, 241, 244
value play(s) . . . . . . . . . . . . . . . . . . . . . . . . . . . . . . . . . . . . . . . . . 74, 77, 78, 99, 100
violations . . . . . . . . . . . . . . . . . . . . . . . . . . . . . . . . . . . . . . . . . . . . . . . . . . . . . 167

## W

wholesalers . . . . . . . . . . . 62, 64, 117, 131, 133, 153, 155, 156, 166, 169, 185, 186, 192–194, 196, 198, 201, 231
wholesaling . . . . . . . . . . . . 132, 148, 151–155, 182, 199–201, 204, 217, 237, 244

## Y

yield play(s) . . . . . . . . . . . . . . . . . . . . . . . . . . . . . . . . . . . . . . . . . . 74, 99, 100, 244

*Index:* R–Y

# Juan Pablo's
## Recommended Reading List

- ✓ *Think and Grow Rich* – by Napoleon Hill
- ✓ *Rich Dad, Poor Dad* – by Robert Kiyosaki
- ✓ *7 Habits of Highly Effective People* – by Stephen Covey
- ✓ *4 Hour Workweek* – by Tim Ferris
- ✓ *5 Easy Steps to Financial Freedom* – Duane Harden
- ✓ The *Bible*